Rifle And Light Infantry Tactics; For The Exercise And Manoeuvers Of Troops When Acting As Light Infantry Or Riflemen

Hardee, William Joseph, 1815-1873

Nabu Public Domain Reprints:

You are holding a reproduction of an original work published before 1923 that is in the public domain in the United States of America, and possibly other countries. You may freely copy and distribute this work as no entity (individual or corporate) has a copyright on the body of the work. This book may contain prior copyright references, and library stamps (as most of these works were scanned from library copies). These have been scanned and retained as part of the historical artifact.

This book may have occasional imperfections such as missing or blurred pages, poor pictures, errant marks, etc. that were either part of the original artifact, or were introduced by the scanning process. We believe this work is culturally important, and despite the imperfections, have elected to bring it back into print as part of our continuing commitment to the preservation of printed works worldwide. We appreciate your understanding of the imperfections in the preservation process, and hope you enjoy this valuable book.

Publishers' Notice.

Supplies of this work from the North having been stopped as contraband of war, this edition is got up for practical purposes and immediate use, in an emergency that admits of no delay; and a considerable portion of remarks and matter, not particularly pertinent has been omitted. The numbering of sections, however, has been retained, which will explain a *hiatus* in numbers, wherever it occurs. The edition has been revised in this manner to subserve the pressing demand of a great exigency, and gives all the drill information imperatively necessary for soldier and officer.

HUTTON & FRELIGH.

RIFLE AND LIGHT INFANTRY TACTICS.

TITLE FIRST.

ARTICLE FIRST.—*Formation of a Regiment in order of battle, or in line.*

1. A regiment is composed of ten companies, which will habitually be posted from right to left, in the following order: first, sixth, fourth, ninth, third, eighth, fifth, tenth, seventh, second, according to the rank of captains

2 With a less number of companies the same principle will be observed, viz the first captain will command the right company, the second captain the left company, the third captain the right center company, and so on.

3. The companies thus posted will be designated from right to left, *first* company, *second* company, &c This designation will be observed in the manœuvres.

4. The first two companies on the right, whatever their denomination, will form the *first division;* the next two companies the *second division*, and so on, to the left.

5 Each company will be divided into two equal parts, which will be designated as the first and second platoon, counting from the right, and each platoon, in like manner, will be subdivided into two sections

6. In all exercises and manœuvres, every regiment, or part of a regiment, composed of two or more companies, will be designated as a battalion.

7 The color, with a guard to be hereinafter designated, will be posted on the left of the right center battalion company That company and all on its right, will be denominated the *right wing* of the battalion, the remaining companies the *left wing.*

8. The formation of a regiment is in two ranks; and each company will be formed into two ranks, in the following manner: the corporals will be posted in the front rank, and on the right and left of platoons, according to hight; the tallest corporal and the tallest man will form the first file, the next two tallest men will form the second file, and so on to the last file, which will be composed of the shortest corporal and the shortest man

9. The odd and even files, numbered as one, two, in the company, from right to left, will form groups of four men, who will be design

FORMATION OF THE BATTALION.

10. The distance from one rank to another will be thirteen inches, measured from the breasts of the rear rank men to the backs or knapsacks of the front rank men.

11. For manœuvring, the companies of a battalion will always be equalized, by transferring men from the strongest to the weakest companies.

Post of Company Officers, Sergeants and Corporals.

12. The company officers and sergeants are nine in number and will be posted in the following manner:

13. The *captain* on the right of the company, touching with the left elbow.

14. The *first sergeant* in the rear rank, touching with the left elbow, and covering the captain. In the manœuvres he will be denominated *covering sergeant*, or *right guide* of the company.

15. The remaining officers and sergeants will be posted as file closers, and two paces behind the rear rank.

16. The *first lieutenant*, opposite the center of the fourth section.

17. The *second lieutenant*, opposite the center of the first platoon.

18. The *third lieutenant*, opposite the center of the second platoon.

19. The *second sergeant*, opposite the second file from the left of the company. In the manœuvres he will be designated *left guide* of the company.

20. The *third sergeant*, opposite the second file from the right of the second platoon.

21. The *fourth sergeant*, opposite the second file from the left of the first platoon.

22. The *fifth sergeant*, opposite the second file from the right of the first platoon.

23. In the left or tenth company of the battalion, the second sergeant will be posted in the front rank, and on the left of the battalion.

24. The corporals will be posted in the front rank, as prescribed No. 8.

25. Absent officers and sergeants will be replaced—officers by sergeants, and sergeants by corporals. The colonel may detach a first lieutenant from one company to command another, of which both the captain and first lieutenant are absent; but this authority will give no right to a lieutenant to demand to be so detached.

Posts of Field Officers and Regimental Staff.

26. The field officers, colonel, lieutenant colonel and major, are supposed to be mounted, and on active service shall be on horseback. The adjutant, when the battalion is manœuvring, will be on foot.

27. The colonel will take post thirty paces in rear of the file closers, and opposite the center of the battalion. This distance will be reduced whenever there is a reduction in the front of the battalion.

28. The lieutenant colonel and the major will be opposite the centers of the right and left wings respectively, and twelve paces in rear of the file closers.

29. The adjutant and sergeant major will be opposite the right and left of the battalion, respectively, and eight paces in rear of the file closers.

30. The adjutant and sergeant major will aid the lieutenant colonel and major, respectively, in the manœuvres.

31. The colonel, if absent, will be replaced by the lieutenant colonel, and the latter by the major. If all the field officers be absent, the senior captain will command the battalion; but if either be present, he will not call the senior captain to act as field officer, except in case of evident necessity.

32. The quarter-master, surgeon, and other staff officers, in one rank, on the left of the colonel, and three paces in his rear.

33. The quarter-master sergeant, on a line with the front rank of the field music, and two paces on the right.

Posts of Field Music and Band.

34. The buglers will be drawn up in four ranks, and posted twelve paces in rear of the file closers, the left opposite the center of the left center company. The senior principal musician will be two paces in front of the field music, and the other two paces in the rear.

35. The regimental band, if there be one, will be drawn up in two or four ranks, according to its numbers, and posted five paces in rear of the field music, having one of the principal musicians at its head.

Color-guard.

36. In each battalion the color-guard will be composed of eight corporals, and posted on the left of the right center company, of which company, for the time being, the guard will make a part.

37. The front rank will be composed of a sergeant, to be selected by the colonel, who will be called, for the time, *color-bearer*, with the two ranking corporals, respectively, on his right and left; the rear rank will be composed of the three corporals next in rank; and the three remaining corporals will be posted in their rear, and on the line of file closers. The left guide of the color-company, when these three last named corporals are in the rank of file closers, will be immediately on their left.

38. In battalions with less than five companies present, there will be no color-guard, and no display of colors, except it may be at reviews.

39. The corporals for the color-guard will be selected from those most distinguished for regularity and precision, as well in their positions under arms as in their marching. The latter advantage, and a [illegible] cularly sought [illegible] bearer

General Guides.

40. There will be two *general* guides in each battalion, selected, for the time, by the colonel, from among the sergeants (other than first sergeants) the most distinguished for carriage under arms, and accuracy in marching

41 These sergeants will be respectively denominated, in the manœuvres, *right general guide,* and *left general guide,* and be posted in the line of file closers, the first in rear of the right, and the second in rear of the left flank of the battalion.

ARTICLE SECOND.— *Instruction of the Battalion*

42. Every commanding officer is responsible for the instruction of his command He will assemble the officers together for theoretical and practical instruction as often as he may judge necessary, and when unable to attend to this duty in person, it will be discharged by the officer next in rank

43 Captains will be held responsible for the theoretical and practical instruction of their non-commissioned officers, and the adjutant for the instruction of the non-commissioned staff. To this end, they will require those tactics to be studied and recited lesson by lesson, and when instruction is given on the ground, each non-commissioned officer, as he explains a movement, should be required to put it into practical operation.

44. The non-commissioned officers should also be practiced in giving commands. Each command, in a lesson, at the theoretical instruction, should first be given by the instructor, and then repeated, in succession, by the non-commissioned officers, so that while they become habituated to the commands, uniformity may be established in the manner of giving them

45 In the school of the soldier, the company officers will be the instructors of the squads, but if there be not a sufficient number of company officers present, intelligent sergeants may be substituted; and two or three squads, under sergeant instructors, be superintended, at the same time, by an officer.

46 In the school of the company, the lieutenant-colonel and the major, under the colonel, will be the principal instructors, substituting frequently the captain of the company, and sometimes one of the lieutenants; the substitute, as far as practicable, being one of the principals

47. In the school of the battalion, the brigadier general may constitute himself the principal instructor, frequently substituting the colonel of the battalion, sometimes the lieutenant colonel or major, and twice or thrice, in the same course of instruction, each of the three senior captains. In this school, also, the substitute will always, if practicable, be superintended by the brigadier general or the colonel, or (in case of a captain being the instructor), by the lieutenant colonel or major.

48. Individual instruction being the basis of the instruction of companies, on which that of the regiment depends, and the first principles having the greatest influence upon this individual instruction, classes of recruits should be watched with the greatest care.

49. Instructors will explain, in a few clear and precise words, the movement to be executed; and not to overburden the memory of the men, they will always use the same terms to explain the same principles.

50. They should often join example to precedent, should keep up the attention of the men by an animated tone, and pass rapidly from one movement to another, as soon as that which they command has been executed in a satisfactory manner.

51. The saber bayonet should only be fixed when required to be used, either for attack or defense; the exercises and manœuvres will be executed without the bayonet.

52. In the movements which require the bayonet to be fixed, the chief of the battalion will cause the signal *to fix bayonet* to be sounded; at this signal the men will fix bayonets without command, and immediately replace their pieces in the position they were before the signal.

Instruction of Officers.

53. The instruction of officers can be perfected only by joining theory to practice. The colonel will often practice them in marching and in estimating distances, and he will carefully endeavor to cause them to take steps equal in length and swiftness. They will also be exercised in the double quick step.

54. The instruction of officers will include all the Titles in this system of drill, and such regulations as prescribe their duties in peace and war.

55. Every officer will make himself perfectly acquainted with the bugle signals; and should, by practice, be enabled, if necessary, to sound them. This knowledge, so necessary in general instruction, becomes of vital importance on actual service in the field.

Instruction of Sergeants.

56. As the discipline and efficiency of a company materially depend on the conduct and character of its sergeants, they should be selected with care, and properly instructed in all the duties appertaining to their rank.

57. Their theoretical instruction should include the School of the Soldier, the School of the Company, and the Drill for Skirmishers. They should likewise know all the details of service, and the regulations prescribing their duties in garrison and in campaign.

58. The captain selects from the corporals in his company those whom he judges fit to be admitted to the theoretical instruction of the sergeants.

Instruction of Corporals.

59. Their theoretical instruction should include the School of the Soldier, and such regulations as prescribe their duties in garrison and in campaign.

60. The captain selects from his company a few privates, who may be admitted to the theoretical instruction of the corporals.

61. As the instruction of sergeants and corporals is intended principally to qualify them for the instruction of the privates, they should be taught not only to execute, but to explain intelligibly everything they may be required to teach.

Commands.

There are three kinds.

62. The command of *caution*, which is *attention*.

63. The *preparatory command*, which indicates the movement which is to be executed.

64. The command of *execution*, such as *march* or *halt*, or, in the manual of arms, the part of command which causes an execution.

65. The tone of the command should be animated, distinct, and of a loudness proportioned to the number of men under instruction.

66. The command *attention* is pronounced at the top of the voice, dwelling on the last syllable.

67. The command of *execution* will be pronounced in a tone firm and brief.

68. The commands of caution and the preparatory commands are herein distinguished by *italics*, those of execution by CAPITALS.

69. Those preparatory commands which, from their length, are difficult to be pronounced at once, must be divided into two or three parts, with an ascending progression in the tone of command, but always in such a manner that the tone of execution may be more energetic and elevated. the divisions are indicated by a hyphen. The parts of commands which are placed in a parenthesis, are not pronounced.

TITLE SECOND—SCHOOL OF THE SOLDIER

General Rules and division of the School of the Soldier.

70. The object of this school being the individual and progressive instruction of the recruits, the instructor never requires a movement to be executed until he has given an exact explanation of it, and he executes, himself, the movement which he commands, so as to join example to precept. He accustoms the recruit to take, by himself, the position which is explained—teaches him to rectify it only when required by his want of intelligence—and sees that all the movements are performed without precipitation.

71. Each movement should be understood before passing to another. After they have been properly executed in the order laid down in each lesson, the instructor no longer confines himself to

that order; on the contrary, he should change it, that he may judge of the intelligence of the men.

72. The instructor allows the men to rest at the end of each part of the lessons, and oftener, if he thinks proper, especially at the commencement, for this purpose he commands REST

73. At the command REST, the soldier is no longer required to preserve immobility, or to remain in his place. If the instructor wishes merely to relieve the attention of the recruit, he commands, *in place*—REST, the soldier is then not required to preserve his immobility, but he always keeps one of his feet in its place

74. When the instructor wishes to commence the instruction, he commands—ATTENTION, at this command the soldier takes his position, remains motionless, and fixes his attention

75 The *School of the Soldier* will be divided into three parts:— the first, comprehending what ought to be taught to recruits without arms; the second the manual of arms, the loadings and firings; the third, the principles of allignment, the march by the front, the different steps, the march by the flank, the principles of wheeling and those of change of direction, also, long marches in double quick time and the run

76 Each part will be divided into lessons, as follows

PART FIRST.

Lesson 1 Position of the soldier without arms, Eyes right, left and front

Lesson 2 Facings

Lesson 3 Principles of the direct step in common and quick time.

Lesson 4. Principles of the direct step in double quick time and the run

PART SECOND

Lesson 1 Principles of shouldered arms

Lesson 2. Manual of arms.

Lesson 3 To load in four times and at will.

Lesson 4. Firings, direct, oblique, by file and by rank

Lesson 5. To fire and load, kneeling and lying.

Lesson 6 Bayonet exercise.

PART THIRD

Lesson 1. Union of eight or twelve men for instruction in the principles of allignment

Lesson 2 The direct march, the oblique march, and the different steps

Lesson 3 The march by the flank.

Lesson 4. Principles of wheeling and change of direction.

Lesson 5. Long marches in double quick time, and the run, with arms and knapsacks

PART FIRST.

77. Th. . . . . a time but thr. . . . . great com-

pared with that of the instructors. In this case the recruits will be placed in a single rank, at one pace from each other. In this part, the recruit will be without arms

LESSON I —*Position of the Soldier*

78 Heels on the same line, as near each other as the conformation of the man will permit,

The feet turned out equally, and forming with each other something less than a right angle,

The knees straight without stiffness;

The body erect on the hips, inclining a little forward,

The shoulders square and falling equally,

The arms hanging naturally,

The elbows near the body,

The palm of the hand turned a little to the front, the little finger behind the seem of the pantaloons,

The head erect and square to the front, without constraint;

The chin near the stock, without covering it,

The eyes fixed straight to the front, and striking the ground about the distance of fifteen paces.

REMARKS ON THE POSITION OF THE SOLDIER

Heels on the same Line,

79. Because, if one were in the rear of the other, the shoulder on that side would be thrown back, or the position of the soldier would be constrained.

Heels more or less closed,

Because, men who are knock-kneed, or who have legs with large calves, cannot, without constraint, make their heels touch while standing

The feet equally turned out, and not forming too large an angle,

Because, if one foot were turned out more than the other, a shoulder would be deranged, and if both feet be too much turned out, it would not be practicable to incline the upper part of the body forward without rendering the whole position unsteady.

Knees extended without stiffness;

Because, if stiffened, constraint and fatigue would be unavoidable.

The body erect on the hips;

Because, it gives equilibrium to the position. The instructor will observe that many recruits have the bad habit of dropping a shoulder, of drawing in a side, or of advancing a hip, particularly the right, when under arms These are defects he will labor to correct.

The upper part of the body inclining forward,

Because, commonly, recruits are disposed to do the reverse, to project the belly and to throw back the shoulders, when they wish to hold themselves erect, from which result great inconveniences in marching. The habit of inclining forward the upper part of the body is so important to contract, that the instructor must enforce it at the beginning, particularly with recruits who have naturally the opposite habit

Shoulders square;

Because, if the shoulders be advanced beyond the line of the breast, and the back arched (the defect called round-shouldered, not uncommon with recruits,) the man cannot align himself, nor use his piece with address. It is important, then, to correct this defect, and necessary to that end that the coat should set easy about the shoulders and arm pits, but in correcting this defect, the instructor should take care that the shoulders be not thrown too much to the rear, which would cause the belly to project, and the small of the back to be curved.

The arms hanging naturally, elbows near the body, the palm of the hand a little turned to the front, the little finger behind the seam of the pantaloons,

Because these positions are equally important to the *shoulder-arms*, and to prevent the man from occupying more space in a rank than is necessary to a free use of the piece, they have, moreover, the advantage of keeping in the shoulders.

The face straight to the front, and without constraint;

Because, if there be stiffness in the latter position, it would communicate itself to the whole of the upper part of the body, embarrass its movements, and give pain and fatigue

Eyes direct to the front.

Because, this is the surest means of maintaining the shoulders in line—an essential object, to be insisted on and attained

80 The instructor having given the recruit the position of the soldier without arms, will now teach him the turning of the head and eyes. He will command.

1. *Eyes*—RIGHT. 2 FRONT.

81. At the word *right*, the recruit will turn the head gently, so as to bring the inner corner of the left eye in a line with the buttons of the coat, the eyes fixed on the line of the eyes of the men in, or supposed to be in, the same rank

82 At the second command, the head will resume the direct or habitual position.

83. The movement of *Eyes*—LEFT will be executed by inverse means.

84. The instructor will take particular care that the movement of the head does not derange the squareness of the shoulders, which will happen if the movement of the former be too sudden.

85 When the instructor wishes the recruit to pass from the state of attention to that of ease, he will command

REST.

86. To cause a resumption of the habitual position, the instructor will command

1. *Attention*. 2 SQUAD

87. At the first word, the recruit will fix his attention, at the second, he will resume the prescribed position with steadiness

LESSON II.—*Facings*

88. Facings to the right or left will be executed in one *time*, or pause. The instructor will command

1 *Squad*. 2. *Right* (or *left*) — FACE

89 At the second command, raise the right foot slightly, turn on the left heel, raising the toes a little, and then replace the right heel by the side of the left, and on the same line.

90. The full face to the rear (or front) will be executed in two *times*, or pauses The instructor will command

1. *Squad*. 2. ABOUT—FACE

91. (*First time*) At the word *about*, the recruit will turn on the left heel, bring the left toe to the front, carry the right foot to the rear, the hollow opposite to, and full three inches from, the left heel, the feet square to each other.

92. (*Second time*.) At the word *face*, the recruit will turn on both heels, raise the toes a little, extend the hams, face to the rear, bringing, at the same time, the right heel by the side of the left.

93 The instructor will take care that these motions do not derange the position of the body

LESSON III — *Principles of the Direct Step*.

94. The length of the direct step, or pace, in common time, will be twenty-eight inches, reckoning from heel to heel, and, in swiftness, at the rate of ninety in a minute.

95 The instructor, seeing the recruit confirmed in his position, will explain to him the principle and mechanism of this step—placing himself six or seven paces from, and facing to the recruit. He will himself execute slowly the step in the way of illustration, and then command.

1. *Squad, forward* 2 *Common time* 3 MARCH.

96 At the first command, the recruit will throw the weight of the body on the right leg, without bending the left knee

97. At the third command, he will smartly, but without a jerk, carry straight forward the left foot twenty-eight inches from the right, the sole near the ground, the ham extended, the toe a little depressed, and, as also the knee, slightly turned out; he will, at the same time, throw the weight of the body forward, and plant flat the left foot, without shock, precisely at the distance where it finds itself from the right when the weight of the body is brought

forward, the whole of which will now rest on the advanced foot. The recruit will next, in like manner, advance the right foot and plant it as above; the heel twenty-eight inches from the heel of the left foot, and thus continue to march without crossing the legs, or striking the one against the other, without turning the shoulders, and preserving always the face direct to the front.

98. When the instructor shall wish to arrest the march, he will command

1 *Squad.* 2 HALT.

99. At the second command, which will be given at the instant when either foot is coming to the ground, the foot in the rear will be brought up and planted by the side of the other, without shock.

100. The instructor will indicate, from time to time, to the recruit, the cadence of the step, by giving the command *one* at the instant of raising a foot, and *two* at the instant it ought to be planted, observing the cadence of ninety steps in a minute. This method will contribute greatly to impress upon the mind the two motions into which the step is naturally divided.

101. Common time will be employed only in the first and second parts of the School of the Soldier. As soon as the recruit has acquired steadiness, has become established in the principles of shouldered arms, and in the mechanism, length and swiftness of the step in common time, he will be practiced only in quick time, the double quick time, and the run.

102. The principles of the step in quick time are the same as for common time, but its swiftness is at the rate of one hundred and ten steps per minute.

103. The instructor wishing the squad to march in quick time, will command

1 *Squad forward.* 2 MARCH.

LESSON IV.—*Principles of the Double Quick Step.*

104. The length of the double quick step is thirty-three inches, and its swiftness at the rate of one hundred and sixty-five steps per minute.

105. The instructor wishing to teach the recruits the principles and mechanism of the double quick step, will command

1 *Double quick step.* 2 MARCH.

106. At the first command, the recruit will raise his hands to a level with his hips, the hands closed, the nails toward the body, the elbows to the rear.

107. At the second command, he will raise to the front his left leg bent in order to give to the knee the greatest elevation, the part of the leg between the knee and the instep verticle, the toe depressed: he will then replace his foot in its former position, with the right leg he will then execute what has just been prescribed for the left, and the alternate movement of the legs will be continu

1 *Squad.* 2. HALT

108. At the second command, the recruit will bring the foot which is raised by the side of the other, and dropping at the same time his hands by his side, will resume the position of the soldier without arms.

109. The instructor placing himself seven or eight paces from, and facing the recruit, will indicate the cadence by the commands, *one* and *two*, given alternately at the instant each foot should be brought to the ground, which at first will be in common time, but its rapidity will be gradually augmented.

110. The recruit being sufficiently established in the principles of this step, the instructor will command

1 *Squad, forward.* 2 *Double quick.* 3. MARCH

111. At the first command, the recruit will throw the weight of his body on the right leg.

112. At the second command, he will place his arms as indicated No 106.

113. At the third command, he will carry forward the left foot, the leg slightly bent, the knee somewhat raised — will plant his left foot, the toe first, thirty-three inches from the right, and with the right foot will then execute what has just been prescribed for the left. This alternate movement of the legs will take place by throwing the weight of the body on the foot that is planted, and by allowing a natural, oscillatory motion to the arms.

114. The double quick step may be executed with different degrees of swiftness. Under urgent circumstances the cadence of this step may be increased to one hundred and eighty per minute. At this rate a distance of four thousand yards would be passed over in about twenty-five minutes.

115. The recruits will be exercised also in running.

116. The principles are the same as for the double quick step, the only difference consisting in a greater degree of swiftness.

117. It is recommended in marching at double quick time, or the run, that the men should breathe as much as possible through the nose, keeping the mouth closed. Experience has proved that, by conforming to this principle, a man can pass over a much longer distance, and with less fatigue.

PART SECOND

GENERAL RULES

118. The instructor will not pass the men to this second part until they shall be well established in the position of the body, and in the manner of marching at the different steps.

119. He will then unite four men, whom he will place in the same rank, elbow to elbow, and instruct them in the position of shouldered arms, as follows

LESSON 1.—*Principles of Shouldered Arms.*

120 The recruit being placed as explained in the first lesson of the first part, the instructor will cause him to bend the right arm slightly, and place the piece in it, in the following manner.

121. The piece in the right hand—the barrel nearly vertical and resting in the hollow of the shoulder—the guard to the front, the arm hanging nearly at its full length near the body, the thumb and fore-finger embracing the guard, the remaining fingers closed together, and grasping the swell of the stock just under the cock, which rests on the little finger.

122 Recruits are frequently seen with natural defects in the conformation of the shoulders, breast and hips These the instructor will labor to correct in the lessons without arms, and afterwards, by steady endeavors, so that the appearance of the pieces, in the same line, may be uniform, and this without constraint to the men in their positions

123. The instructor will have occasion to remark that recruits, on first bearing arms, are liable to derange their position by lowering the right shoulder and the right hand, or by sinking the hip and spreading out the elbows.

124 He will be careful to correct all these faults by continually rectifying the position, he will sometimes take away the piece to replace it the better, he will avoid fatiguing the recruits too much in the evening, but labor by degrees to render this position so natural and easy that they may remain in it a long time without fatigue

125. Finally, the instructor will take great care that the piece, at a shoulder, be not carried too high nor too low. if too high, the right elbow would spread out, the soldier would occupy too much space in his rank, and the piece be made to waver; if too low, the files would be too much closed, the soldier would not have the necessary space to handle his piece with facility, the right arm would become too much fatigued, and would draw down the shoulder.

126 The instructor, before passing to the second lesson, will cause to be repeated the movements of *eyes right*, *left*, and *front*, and the *facings*.

LESSON II —*Manual of Arms*

127 The manual of arms will be taught to four men, placed, at first, in one rank, elbow to elbow, and afterwards in two ranks

128. Each command will be executed in one *time* (or pause), but this time will be divided into motions, the better to make known the mechanism

129. The rate (or swiftness) of each motion, in the manual of arms, with the exceptions herein indicated, is fixed at the ninetieth part of a minute; but, in order not to fatigue the attention, the instructor will, at first, look more particularly to the execution of the motions, with a strict observance of the cadence,

to which he will bring the recruits progressively, and after they shall have become a little familiarized with the handling of the piece

130 As the motions relative to the cartridge, to the rammer, and to the fixing and unfixing of the bayonet, cannot be executed at the rate prescribed, nor even with a uniform swiftness, they will not be subjected to that cadence. The instructor will, however, labor to cause these motions to be executed with promptness, and, above all, with regularity.

131 The last syllable of the command will decide the brisk execution of the first motion of each time (or pause) The commands *two, three,* and *four,* will decide the brisk execution of the other motions. As soon as the recruits shall well comprehend the positions of the several motions of a time, they will be taught to execute the time without resting on its different motions, the mechanism of the time will nevertheless be observed, as well to give a perfect use of the piece, as to avoid the sinking of, or slurring over, either of the motions

132. The manual of arms will be taught in the following progression: The instructor will command.

Support—Arms.

One time and three motions

133. (*First motion*) Bring the piece, with the right hand, perpendicularly to the front and between the eyes, the barrel to the rear, seize the piece with the left hand at the lower band, raise this hand as high as the chin, and seize the piece at the same time with the right hand four inches below the cock

134 (*Second motion.*) Turn the piece with the right hand, the barrel to the front: carry the piece to the left shoulder, and pass the fore-arm extended on the breast between the right hand and the cock, support the cock against the left fore-arm, the left hand resting on the right breast

135 (*Third motion*) Drop the right hand by the side

136. When the instructor may wish to give repose in this position, he will command·

Rest

137 At this command, the recruits will bring up smartly the right hand to the handle of the piece (small of the stock), when they will not be required to preserve silence, or steadiness of position

138 When the instructor may wish the recruits to pass from this position to that of silence and steadiness, he will command

1 *Attention* 2 Squad

139 At the second word, the recruits will resume the position of the third motion of *support arms*

Shoulder—Arms

One time and three motions

140. (*First motion.*) Grasp the piece with the right hand under and against the left fore-arm; seize it with the left hand at the lower band, the thumb extended, detatch the piece slightly from the shoulder, the left fore-arm along the stock.

141. (*Second motion.*) Carry the piece vertically to the right shoulder with both hands, the rammer to the front, change the position of the right hand so as to embrace the guard with the thumb and fore-finger, slip the left hand to the hight of the shoulder, the fingers extended and joined, the right arm nearly straight.

142. (*Third motion.*) Drop the left hand quickly by the side.

Present—Arms

One time and two motions.

143. (*First motion.*) With the right hand bring the piece erect before the center of the body, the rammer to the front; at the same time seize the piece with the left hand half-way between the guide sight and lower band, the thumb extended along the barrel and against the stock, the fore-arm horizontal and resting against the body, the hand as high as the elbow.

144. (*Second motion.*) Grasp the small of the stock with the right hand below and against the guard.

Shoulder—Arms.

One time and two motions.

145. (*First motion.*) Bring the piece to the right shoulder, at the same time change the position of the right hand so as to embrace the guard with the thumb and fore-finger, slip up the left hand to the hight of the shoulder, the fingers extended and joined, the right arm nearly straight.

146. (*Second motion.*) Drop the left hand quickly by the side.

Order—Arms

One time and two motions.

147. (*First motion.*) Seize the piece briskly with the left hand near the upper band, and detatch it slightly from the shoulder with the right hand, loosen the grasp of the right hand, lower the piece with the left, reseize the piece with the right hand above the lower band, the little finger in rear of the barrel, the butt about four inches from the ground, the right hand supported against the hip, drop the left hand by the side.

148. (*Second motion.*) Let the piece slip through the right hand to the ground by opening slightly the fingers, and take the position about to be described.

Position of order arm.

149. The hand low the barrel between the thumb and fore-

finger extended along the stock; the other fingers extended and joined; the muzzle about two inches from the right shoulder; the rammer in front, the toe (or beak) of the butt, against, and in a line with, the toe of the right foot, the barrel perpendicular

150. When the instructor may wish to give repose in this position, he will command

REST.

151. At this command, the recruits will not be required to preserve silence or steadiness

152. When the instructor may wish the recruits to pass from this position to that of silence and steadiness, he will command:

1 *Attention.* 2. SQUAD

153. At the second word, the recruits will resume the position of *order arms*

Shoulder—ARMS

One time and two motions

154. (*First motion*) Raise the piece vertically with the right hand to the hight of the right breast, and opposite the shoulder, the elbow close to the body, seize the piece with the left hand below the right, and drop quickly the right hand to grasp the piece at the swell of the stock, the thumb and fore-finger embracing the guard; press the piece against the shoulder with the left hand, the right arm nearly straight

155 (*Second motion*) Drop the left hand quickly by the side.

Load in nine times.

*1. LOAD

156. Grasp the piece with the left hand as high as the right elbow, and bring it vertically opposite the middle of the body, shift the right hand to the upper band, place the butt between the feet, the barrel to the front, seize it with the left hand near the muzzle, which should be three inches from the body, carry the right hand to the cartridge box.

2 *Handle*—CARTRIDGE

One time and one motion.

157 Sieze the cartridge with the thumb and next two fingers, and place it between the teeth.

3 *Tear*—CARTRIDGE.

One time and one motion.

158. Tear the paper to the powder, hold the cartridge upright between the thumb and first two fingers, near the top, in this po-

---

*Whenever the loadings and firings are to be executed, the instructor will cause the cartridge box to be brought to the front.

sition place it in front of and near the muzzle—the back of the hand to the front

4 *Charge*—CARTRIDGE

One time and one motion.

159. Empty the powder into the barrel; disengage the ball from the paper with the right hand and the thumb and first two fingers of the left, insert it into the bore, the pointed end uppermost, and press it down with the right thumb; seize the head of the rammer with the thumb and fore-finger of the right hand, the other fingers closed, the elbows near the body

5 *Draw*—RAMMER.

One time and three motions

160 (*First motion*) Half draw the rammer by extending the right arm, steady it in this position with the left thumb, grasp the rammer near the muzzle with the right hand, the little finger uppermost, the nails to the front, the thumb extended along the rammer

161 (*Second motion*) Clear the rammer from the pipes by again extending the arm, the rammer in the prolongation of the pipes

162 (*Third motion*) Turn the rammer, the little end of the rammer passing near the left shoulder, place the head of the rammer on the ball, the back of the hand to the front.

6 *Ram*—CARTRIDGE

One time and one motion.

163 Insert the rammer as far as the right, and steady it in this position with the thumb of the left hand, seize the rammer at the small end with the thumb and fore-finger of the right hand, the back of the hand to the front, press the ball home, the elbows near the body

7 *Return*—RAMMER

One time and three motions

164 (*First motion*) Draw the rammer half-way out, and steady it in this position with the left thumb, grasp it near the muzzle with the right hand, the little finger uppermost, the nails to the front, the thumb along the rammer, clear the rammer from the bore by extending the arm, the nails to the front, the rammer in the prolongation of the bore

165 (*Second motion*) Turn the rammer, the head of the rammer passing near the left shoulder, and insert it in the pipes until the right hand reaches the muzzle, the nails to the front

166 (*Third motion*) Force the rammer home by placing the little fi   .   . ( )at   .   puts th o
left ha   .   ır   w out de-
pressin .

8. PRIME*—*One time and two motions.*

167. (*First motion.*) With the left hand raise the piece till the hand is as high as the eye, grasp the small of the stock with the right hand, half face to the right; place, at the same time, the right foot behind and at right angles with the left, the hollow of the right foot against the left heel. Slip the left hand down to the lower band, the thumb along the stock, the left elbow against the body, bring the piece to the right side, the butt below the right fore-arm—the small of the stock against the body and two inches below the right breast, the barrel upwards, the muzzle on a level with the eye

168. (*Second motion.*) Half cock with the thumb of the right hand, the fingers supported against the guard and the small of the stock—remove the old cap with one of the fingers of the right hand, and with the thumb and fore-finger of the same hand take a cap from the pouch, place it on the nipple, and press it down with the thumb; seize the small of the stock with the right hand.

9. *Shoulder—*ARMS

One time and two motions

169. (*First motion.*) Bring the piece to the right shoulder and support it there with the left hand, face to the front, bring the right heel to the side of and on a line with the left, grasp the piece with the right hand as indicated in the position of *shoulder arms*

170. (*Second motion.*) Drop the left hand quickly by the side

READY

One time and three motions

171. (*First motion.*) Raise the piece slightly with the right hand, making a half face to the right on the left heel, carry the right foot to the rear, and place it at right angles to the left, the hollow of it opposite to, and against the left heel; grasp the piece with the left hand at the lower band and detach it slightly from the shoulder.

172. (*Second motion.*) Bring down the piece with both hands, the barrel upwards, the left thumb extended along the stock, the butt below the right fore-arm, the small of the stock against the body and two inches below the right breast, the muzzle as high as the eye, the left elbow against the side, place at the same time the right thumb on the head of the cock, the other fingers under and against the guard

---

*If Maynard's primer be used, the command will be *load in eight times*, and the eighth command will be, *shoulder arms*, and executed from *return rammer*, in one time and two motions, as follows:

(*First motion.*) Raise the piece with the left hand, and take the position of shoulder arms, as indicated No 146.

(*Second motion.*) Drop the left hand quickly by the side.

173. (*Third motion.*) Cock, and seize the piece at the small of the stock without deranging the position of the butt

AIM.

One time and one motion

174. Raise the piece with both hands, and support the butt against the right shoulder, the left elbow down, the right as high as the shoulder; incline the head upon the butt, so that the right eye may perceive quickly the notch of the hausse, the front sight, and the object aimed at, the left eye closed, the right thumb extended along the stock, the fore-finger on the trigger.

175. When recruits are formed in two ranks to execute the firings, the front rank men will raise a little less the right elbow, in order to facilitate the aim of the rear rank men

176. The rear rank men, in aiming, will each carry the right foot about ten inches to the right, and towards the left heel of the man next on the right, inclining the upper part of the body forward.

FIRE

One time and one motion.

177. Press the fore-finger against the trigger, fire, without lowering or turning the head, and remain in this position

178. Instructors will be careful to observe when the men fire, that they aim at some distinct object, and that the barrel be so directed that the line of fire and the line of sight be in the same vertical plane. They will often cause the firing to be executed on ground of different inclinations, in order to accustom the men to fire at objects either above or below them

LOAD

One time and one motion

179. Bring down the piece with both hands, at the same time face to the front and take the position of *load* as indicated No. 156 Each rear rank man will bring his right foot by the side of the left.

180. The men being in this position, the instructor will cause the loading to be continued by the commands and means prescribed No 156 and following.

181. If, after firing, the instructor should not wish the recruits to reload, he will command :

Shoulder—ARMS

One time and one motion

182. Throw up the piece briskly with the left hand and resume the position of *shoulder arms*, at the same time face to the front, turning on the left heel, and bring the right heel on a line with the left

183. To accustom the recruits to wait for the command *fire*, the instructor, when they are in the position of *aim*, will command:

Recover—ARMS.

One time and one motion

184. At the first part of the command, withdraw the finger from the trigger; at the command *arms*, retake the position of the third motion of *ready*.

185. The recruits being in the position of the third motion of *ready*, if the instructor should wish to bring them to a shoulder, he will command:

Shoulder—ARMS.

One time and one motion

186. At the command *shoulder*, place the thumb upon the cock, the fore-finger on the trigger, half-cock, and seize the small of the stock with the right hand. At the command *arms*, bring up the piece briskly to the right shoulder, and retake the position of shoulder arms.

187. The recruits being at shoulder arms, when the instructor shall wish to fix bayonets, he will command:

Fix—BAYONET.

One time and three motions

188. (*First motion.*) Grasp the piece with the left hand at the hight of the shoulder, and detach it slightly from the shoulder with the right hand.

189. (*Second motion.*) Quit the piece with the right hand, lower it with the left hand, opposite the middle of the body, and place the butt between the feet without shock; the rammer to the rear, the barrel vertical, the muzzle three inches from the body; seize it with the right hand at the upper band, and carry the left hand reversed to the handle of the sabre-bayonet.

190. (*Third motion.*) Draw the sabre-bayonet from the scabbard and fix it on the extremity of the barrel; seize the piece with the left hand, the arm extended, the right hand at the upper band.

Shoulder—ARMS

One time and two motions

191. (*First motion.*) Raise the piece with the left hand and place it against the right shoulder, the rammer to the front; seize the piece at the same time with the right hand at the swell of the stock, the thumb and fore-finger embracing the guard, the right arm nearly extended.

192. (*Second motion.*) Drop briskly the left hand by the side.

Charge—BAYONET.

One time and two motions

193. (*First motion.*) Raise the piece slightly with the right hand

and make a half face to the right on the left heel, place the hollow of the right foot opposite to, and three inches from the left heel, the feet square, seize the piece at the same time with the left hand a little above the lower band

194. (*Second motion.*) Bring down the piece with both hands, the barrel uppermost, the left elbow against the body; seize the small of the stock, at the same time, with the right hand, which will be supported against the hip, the point of the sabre-bayonet as high as the eye

Shoulder—Arms.
One time and two motions.

195. (*First motion.*) Throw up the piece briskly with the left hand in facing to the front, place it against the right shoulder, the rammer to the front, turn the right hand so as to embrace the guard, slide the left hand to the hight of the shoulder, the right hand nearly extended

196. (*Second motion.*) Drop the left hand smartly by the side.

Trail—Arms.
One time and two motions.

197. (*First motion.*) The same as the first motion of *order arms*.

198. (*Second motion.*) Incline the muzzle slightly to the front, the butt to the rear and about four inches from the ground. The right hand supported at the hip, will so hold the piece that the rear rank men may not touch with their bayonets the men in the front rank.

Shoulder—Arms

199. At the command *shoulder*, raise the piece perpendicularly in the right hand, the little finger in rear of the barrel; at the command *arms*, execute what has been prescribed for the *shoulder* from the position of *order arms*

Unfix—Bayonet.
One time and three motions

200. (*First and second motions.*) The same as the first and second motions of *fix bayonet*, except that, at the end of the second command, the thumb of the right hand will be placed on the spring of the sabre-bayonet, and the left hand will embrace the handle of the sabre-bayonet and the barrel, the thumb extended along the blade.

201. (*Third motion.*) Press the thumb of the right hand on the spring, wrest off the sabre-bayonet, turn it to the right, the edge to the front, lower the guard until it touches the right hand, which will seize the back and the edge of the blade between the thumb and first two fingers, the other fingers holding the piece, change the position of the hand without quitting the handle, return the sabre-bayonet to the scabbard, and seize the piece with the left hand, the arm extended.

Shoulder—Arms

One time and two motions

202. (*First motion*.) The same as the first motion from *fix bayonet*, No 191

203. (*Second motion*.) The same as the second motion from *fix bayonet*, No. 192

Secure—Arms

One time and three motions

204. (*First motion*) The same as the first motion of *support arms*, No 133, except with the right hand seize the piece at the small of the stock.

205. (*Second motion*) Turn the piece with both hands, the barrel to the front; bring it opposite the left shoulder, the butt against the hip, the left hand at the lower band, the thumb as high as the chin and extended on the rammer; the piece erect and detached from the shoulder, the left fore-arm against the piece.

206. (*Third motion*.) Reverse the piece, pass it under the left arm, the left hand remaining at the lower band, the thumb on the rammer to prevent it from sliding out, the little finger resting against the hip, the right hand falling at the same time by the side

Shoulder—Arms

One time and three motions

207. (*First motion*) Raise the piece with the left hand, and seize it with the right hand at the small of the stock. The piece erect and detached from the shoulder, the butt against the hip, the left fore-arm along the piece.

208. (*Second motion*.) The same as the second motion of *shoulder arms from a support*.

209. (*Third motion*) The same as the third motion of *shoulder arms from a support*

Right shoulder shift—Arms.

One time and two motions

210. (*First motion*.) Detach the piece perpendicularly from the shoulder with the right hand, and seize it with the left between the lower band and guide-sight, raise the piece, the left hand at the hight of the shoulder and four inches from it; place, at the same time, the right hand on the butt, the beak between the first two fingers, the other two fingers under the butt plate

211. (*Second motion*) Quit the piece with the left hand, raise and place the piece on the right shoulder with the right hand, the lock plate upwards, let fall, at the same time, the left hand by the side.

Shoulder—Arms.

One time and two motions.

212. (*First motion*) Raise the piece perpendicularly by extend-

ing the right arm to its full length, the rammer to the front, at the same time seize the piece with the left hand between the lower band and guide sight.

213 (*Second motion.*) Quit the butt with the right hand, which will immediately embrace the guard, lower the piece to the position of shoulder arms, slide up the left hand to the hight of the shoulder, the fingers extended and closed. Drop the left hand by the side

214. The men being at support arms, the instructor will sometimes cause pieces to be brought to the right shoulder. To this effect, he will command:

Right shoulder shift—ARMS

One time and two motions

215. (*First motion.*) Seize the piece with the right hand, below and near the left fore-arm, place the left hand under the butt, the heel of the butt between the first two fingers

216. (*Second motion.*) Turn the piece with the left hand, the lock plate upwards, carry it to the right shoulder, the left hand still holding the butt, the muzzle elevated; hold the piece in this position and place the right hand upon the butt as is prescribed No 210, and let fall the left hand by the side

Support—ARMS.

One time and two motions

217 (*First motion.*) The same as the first motion of *shoulder arms*, No 212

218 (*Second motion.*) Turn the piece with both hands, the barrel to the front, carry it opposite the left shoulder, slip the right hand to the small of the stock, place the left fore-arm extended on the breast as is prescribed No 134, and let fall the right hand by the side.

Arms—AT WILL

One time and one motion

219 At this command, carry the piece at pleasure on either shoulder, with one or both hands, the muzzle elevated

Shoulder—ARMS

One time and one motion

220. At this command, retake quickly the position of shoulder arms

221. The recruits being at ordered arms, when the instructor shall wish to cause the pieces to be placed on the ground, he will command:

Ground—ARMS.

One time and two motions.

222 (F   bar-

rel to the left; at the same time seize the cartridge box with the left hand, bend the body, advance the left foot, the heel opposite the lower band; lay the piece on the ground with the right hand, the toe of the butt on a line with the right toe, the knees slightly bent, the right heel raised.

223. (*Second motion.*) Rise up, bring the left foot by the side of the right, quit the cartridge box with the left hand, and drop the hands by the side.

Raise—ARMS.

One time and two motions.

224. (*First motion.*) Seize the cartridge box with the left hand, bend the body, advance the left foot opposite the lower band, and seize the piece with the right hand.

225. (*Second motion.*) Raise the piece, bringing the left foot by the side of the right; turn the piece with the right hand, the rammer to the front; at the same time quit the cartridge box with the left hand, and drop this hand by the side.

Inspection of Arms.

226. The recruits being at *ordered arms*, and having the sabre-bayonet in the scabbard, if the instructor wishes to cause an inspection of arms, he will command:

Inspection—ARMS.

One time and two motions.

227. (*First motion.*) Seize the piece with the left hand below and near the upper band, carry it with both hands opposite the middle of the body, the butt between the feet, the rammer to the rear, the barrel vertical, the muzzle about three inches from the body; carry the left hand reversed to the sabre bayonet, draw it from the scabbard and fix it on the barrel; grasp the piece with the left hand below and near the upper band, seize the rammer with the thumb and fore-finger of the right hand bent, the other fingers closed.

228. (*Second motion.*) Draw the rammer as has been explained in *loading*, and let it glide to the bottom of the bore, replace the piece with the left hand opposite the right shoulder, and retake the position of *ordered arms*.

229. The instructor will then inspect in succession the piece of each recruit, in passing along the front of the rank. Each, as the instructor reaches him, will raise smartly his piece with his right hand, seize it with the left between the lower band and guide sight the lock to the front, the left hand at the hight of the chin the piece opposite to the left eye; the instructor will take it with the right hand at the handle, and, after inspecting it, will return it to the recruit, who will receive it back with the right hand, and replace it in the position of *ordered arms*.

230. When the instructor shall have passed him, each recru

will retake the position prescribed at the command *inspection arms*, return the rammer, and resume the position of *ordered arms*.

231. If, instead of *inspection of arms*, the instructor should merely wish to cause bayonets to be fixed, he will command:

Fix—BAYONET.

232. Take the position indicated in No. 227, fix bayonets as has been explained, and immediately resume the position of *ordered arms*.

233. If it be the wish of the instructor, after firing, to ascertain whether the pieces have been discharged, he will command:

Spring—RAMMERS.

234. Put the rammer in the barrel as has been explained above, and immediately retake the position of *ordered arms*.

235. The instructor, for the purpose stated, can take the rammer by the small end, and spring it in the barrel, or cause each recruit to make it ring in the barrel.

236. Each recruit, after the instructor passes him, will return rammer and resume the position of *ordered arms*.

Remarks on the Manual of Arms.

237. The manual of arms frequently distorts the persons of recruits before they acquire ease and confidence in the several positions. The instructor will therefore frequently recur to elementary principles in the course of the lessons.

238. Recruits are also extremely liable to curve the sides and back, and to derange the shoulders, especially in loading. Consequently, the instructor will not cause them to dwell too long at a time in one position.

239. When, after some days of exercise in the manual of arms, the four men shall be well established in their use, the instructor will always terminate the lesson by marching the men for some time in one rank, and at one pace apart, in common and quick time, in order to confirm them more and more in the mechanism of the step; he will also teach them to mark time and to change step; which will be executed in the following manner:

To mark time.

240. The four men marching in the direct step, the instructor will command:

1. *Mark time.* 2. MARCH.

241. At the second command, which will be given at the instant a foot is coming to the ground, the recruits will make a semblance of marching, by bringing the heels by the side of each other, and observing the cadence of the step, by raising each foot alternately without advancing.

242. The instructor wishing the direct step to be resumed, will command:

1 *Forward*   2 MARCH

243. At the second command, which will be given as prescribed above, the recruits will retake the step of twenty-eight inches

To change step

244 The squad being in march, the instructor will command

1. *Change step*   2 MARCH

245. At the second command, which will be given at the instant either foot is coming to the ground, bring the foot which is in rear by the side of that which is in front, and step off again with the foot which was in front.

To march backwards

246. The instructor wishing the squad to march backwards, will command

1 *Squad backward*   2 MARCH

247 At the second command, the recruits will step off smartly with the left foot fourteen inches to the rear, reckoning from heel to heel, and so on with the feet in succession till the command *halt*, which will always be preceded by the caution *squad*. The men will halt at this command, and bring back the foot in front by the side of the other

248 This step will always be executed in quick time

249 The instructor will be watchful that the recruits march straight to the rear, and that the erect position of the body and the piece be not deranged.

LESSON III.—*To load in four times.*

250 The object of this lesson is to prepare the recruits to load at will, and to cause them to distinguish the times which require the greatest regularity and attention, such as *charge cartridge, ram cartridge* and *prime*. It will be divided as follows.

251 The first time will be executed at the end of the command, the three others at the commands, *two, three* and *four*.

The instructor will command

1. *Load in four times.*   2 LOAD

252 Execute the times to include charge cartridge.

TWO.

253 Execute the times to include ram cartridge

THREE

254. Execute the times to include prime

FOUR

255. Execute the time of shoulder arms.

To load at will

256. The instructor will next teach loading at will, which will

SCHOOL OF THE SOLDIER.

be executed as loading in four times, but continued, and without resting on either of the times. He will command

1 *Load at will.* 2 LOAD

257. The instructor will habituate the recruits, by degrees, to load with the greatest possible promptitude, each without regulating himself by his neighbor, and above all without waiting for him.

258. The cadence prescribed No 129, is not applicable to loading in four times, or at will.

LESSON IV.—*Firings.*

259. The firings are direct or oblique, and will be executed as follows

The direct fire

260. The instructor will give the following commands:

1 *Fire by squad* 2. *Squad* 3 READY 4 AIM. 5. FIRE 6 LOAD

261. These several commands will be executed as has been prescribed in the *Manual of Arms* At the third command, the men will come to the position of *ready* as heretofore explained At the fourth they will aim according to the rank in which each may find himself placed, the rear rank men inclining forward a little the upper part of the body, in order that their pieces may reach as much beyond the front rank as possible

262. At the sixth command they will load their pieces and return immediately to the position of *ready*

263. The instructor will recommence the firing by the command

1. *Squad* 2 AIM. 3. FIRE. 4. LOAD.

164 When the instructor wishes the firing to cease, he will command

Cease firing

265 At this command the men will cease firing, but will load their pieces if unloaded, and afterwards bring them to a shoulder

Oblique firings

266 The oblique firings will be executed to the right and left, and by the same commands as the direct fire, with this single difference—the command *aim* will always be preceded by the caution, *right* or *left oblique*

Position of the two ranks in the Oblique Fire to the right

267. At the command *ready*, the two ranks will execute what has been prescribed for the direct fire

268. At the cautionary command, *right oblique*, the two ranks will throw back the right shoulder and look steadily at the object to be hit

269. At the command, *aim*, each front rank man will aim to the right without deranging the feet; each rear rank man will advance the left foot about eight inches toward the right heel of the man next on the right of his file leader and aim to the right, inclining the upper part of the body forward and bending a little the left knee.

Position of the two ranks in the Oblique Fire to the left.

270. At the cautionary command, *left oblique*, the two ranks will throw back the left shoulder and look steadily at the object to be hit.

271. At the command, *aim*, the front rank will take aim to the left without deranging the feet; each man in the rear will advance the right foot about eight inches toward the right heel of the man next on the right of his file leader, and aim to the left, inclining the upper part of the body forward and bending a little the right knee.

272. In both cases, at the command, *load*, the men of each rank will come to the position of load as prescribed in the direct fire; the rear rank men bringing back the foot which is to the right and front by the side of the other. Each man will continue to load as if isolated.

To fire by file.

273. The fire by file will be executed by the two ranks, the files of which will fire successively, and without regulating on each other, except for the first fire.

274. The instructor will command:

1. *Fire by file.* 2. *Squad.* 3. READY. 4. COMMENCE FIRING.

275. At the third command, the two ranks will take the position prescribed in the direct fire.

276. At the fourth command, the file on the right will aim and fire; the rear rank man in aiming will take the position indicated No. 176.

277. The men of this file will load their pieces briskly and fire a second time; reload and fire again, and so on in continuation.

278. The second file will aim at the instant the first brings down pieces to reload, and will conform in all respects to that which has just been prescribed for the first file.

279. After the first fire, the front and rear rank men will not be required to fire at the same time.

280. Each man, after loading, will return to the position of ready, and continue the fire.

281. When the instructor wishes the fire to cease, he will command:

Cease—FIRING.

282. At this command, the men will cease firing. If they have fired they will load their pieces and bring them to a shoulder; if at the position of *ready*, they will half-cock and shoulder arms. If in the position of *aim*, they will bring down their pieces, half-cock, and shoulder arms.

SCHOOL OF THE SOLDIER.

To fire by rank.

283. The fire by rank will be executed by each entire rank, alternately.

284. The instructor will command:

1. *Fire by rank.* 2. *Squad.* 3. READY. 4. *Rear Rank.* 5. AIM. 6. FIRE. 7. LOAD.

285. At the third command, the two ranks will take the position of *ready*, as prescribed in the direct fire.

286. At the seventh command, the rear rank will execute that which has been prescribed in the direct fire, and afterwards take the position of *ready*.

287. As soon as the instructor sees several men of the rear rank in the position of ready, he will command:

1. *Front Rank.* 2. AIM. 3. FIRE. 4. LOAD.

288. At these commands, the men in the front rank will execute what has been prescribed for the rear rank, but they will not step off with right foot.

289. The instructor will recommence the firing by the rear rank, and will thus continue to alternate from rank to rank, until he shall wish the firing to cease, when he will command, *cease firing*, which will be executed as heretofore prescribed.

LESSON V.—*To fire and load kneeling.*

290. In this exercise the squad will be supposed loaded and drawn up in one rank. The instruction will be given to each man individually, without times or motions, and in the following manner.

291. The instructor will command:

FIRE AND LOAD KNEELING.

292. At this command, the man on the right of the squad will move forward three paces and halt; then carry the right foot to the rear and to the right of the left heel, and in a position convenient for placing the right knee upon the ground in bending the left leg; place the right knee upon the ground; lower the piece, the left fore-arm supported upon the thigh on the same side, the right hand on the small of the stock, the butt resting on the right thigh, the left hand supporting the piece near the lower band.

293. He will next move the right leg to the left around the knee supported on the ground, until this leg is nearly perpendicular to the direction of the left foot, and thus seat himself comfortably on the right heel.

294. Raise the piece with the right hand and support it with the left, holding it near the lower band, the left elbow resting on the left thigh near the knee; seize the hammer with the thumb, the fore-finger under the guard, cock, and seize the piece at the small of the st

295. Bring the piece down as soon as it is fired, and support it with the left hand, the butt resting against the right thigh; carry the piece to the rear rising on the knee, the barrel downwards, the butt resting on the ground; in this position support the piece with the left hand at the upper band, draw cartridge with the right and load the piece, ramming the ball, if necessary, with both hands.

296. When loaded bring the piece to the front with the left hand, which holds it at the upper band; seize it at the same time with the right hand at the small of the stock; turn the piece, the barrel uppermost and nearly horizontal, the left elbow resting on the left thigh; half-cock, remove the old cap and prime, rise, and return to the ranks.

297. The second man will then be taught what has just been prescribed for the first, and so on through the remainder of the squad.

Fire and load lying.

298. In this exercise the squad will be in one rank and loaded: the instruction will be given individually and without times or motions.

299. The instructor will command:

Fire and load lying.

300. At this command, the man on the right of the squad will move forward three paces and halt; he will then bring his piece to an order, drop on both knees, and place himself on the ground flat on his belly. In this position he will support the piece nearly horizontal with the left hand, holding it near the lower band, the butt end of the piece and the left elbow resting on the ground, the barrel uppermost; cock the piece with the right hand, and carry this hand to the small of the stock; raise the piece with both hands, press the butt against the shoulder, and resting on both elbows, *aim* and *fire*.

301. As soon as he has fired, bring the piece down and turn upon his left side, still resting on his left elbow; bring back the piece until the cock is opposite his breast, the butt end resting on the ground; take out a cartridge with the right hand; seize the small of the stock with this hand, holding the cartridge with the thumb and two first fingers; he will then throw himself on his back still holding the piece with both hands; carry the piece to the rear, place the butt between the heels, the barrel up, the muzzle elevated. In this position, charge cartridge, draw rammer, ram cartridge, and return rammer.

302. When finished loading, the man will turn again upon his left side, remove the old cap and prime, then raise the piece vertically, rise, turn about, and resume his position in the ranks.

303. The second man will be taught what has just been prescribed for the first, and so on throughout the squad.

Lesson VI.—*Bayonet Exercise*

304. The bayonet exercise in this book will be confined to two movements, the *guard against infantry*, and the *guard against cavalry*. The men will be placed in one rank, with two paces interval, and being at shoulder arms, the instructor will command:

1. *Guard against Infantry.* 2. GUARD

One time and two motions

305. (*First motion.*) Make a half face to the right, turning on both heels, the feet square to each other; at the same time raise the piece slightly, and seize it with the left hand above and near the lower band

306 (*Second motion.*) Carry the right foot twenty inches perpendicularly to the rear, the right heel on the prolongation of the left, the knees slightly bent, the weight of the body resting equally on both legs; lower the piece with both hands, the barrel uppermost, the left elbow against the body, seize the piece at the same time with the right hand at the small of the stock, the arms falling naturally, the point of the bayonet slightly elevated.

Shoulder—ARMS

One time and one motion.

307 Throw up the piece with the left hand, and place it against the right shoulder, at the same time bring the right heel by the side of the left and face to the front

1. *Guard against Cavalry* 2 GUARD

One time and two motions

308 Both motions the same as for *guard against infantry*, except that the right hand will be supported against the hip, and the bayonet held at the hight of the eye, as in *charge bayonet*.

Shoulder—ARMS

One time and one motion.

309. Spring up the piece with the left hand and place it against the right shoulder, at the same time bring the right heel by the side of the left, and face to the front.

PART THIRD.

310 When the recruits are well established in the *principles and mechanism of the step, the position of the body*, and *the manual of arms*, the instructor will unite eight men, at least, and twelve men, at most, in order to teach them the principles of alignment, the principles of the touch of elbows in marching to the front, the principles of the march by the flank wheeling from a halt, wheeling in marching and the change of direction to the side of the

guide. He will place the squad in one rank elbow to elbow, and number the men from right to left.

Lesson I.—*Alignments.*

311. The instructor will at first teach the recruits to align themselves man by man, in order the better to make them comprehend the principles of alignment; to this end, he will command the two men on the right flank to march two paces to the front, and having aligned them, he will caution the remainder of the squad to move up, as they may be successively called, each by his number, and align themselves successively on the line of the first two men.

312. Each recruit, as designated by his number, will turn the head and eyes to the right as prescribed in the first lesson of the first part, and will march in *quick time two paces forward*, shortening the last, so as to find himself about six inches behind the new alignment, which he ought never to pass; he will next move up steadily by steps of two or three inches, the hams extended, to the side of the man next to him on the alignment, so that, without deranging the head, the line of the eyes, or that of the shoulders, he may find himself in the exact line of his neighbor, whose elbow he will lightly touch without opening his own.

313. The instructor seeing the rank well aligned, will command:

Front.

314. At this, the recruits will turn eyes to the front, and remain firm.

315. Alignments to the left will be executed on the same principles.

316. When the recruits shall have thus learned to align themselves man by man, correctly, and without groping or jostling, the instructor will cause the entire rank to align itself at once by the command:

Right (or *left*)—Dress.

317. At this, the rank, except the two men placed in advance as a basis of alignment, will move up in *quick time*, and place themselves on the new line, according to the principles prescribed No. 312.

318. The instructor, placed five or six paces in front, and facing the rank, will carefully observe that the principles are followed, and then pass to the flank that has served as the basis, to verify the alignment.

319. The instructor seeing the greater number of the rank aligned, will command:

Front.

320. The instructor may afterwards order *this* or *that* file *forward* or *back*, designating each by its number. The file or files designated, only, will slightly turn the head towards the basis, to judge how much they ought to move up or back, steadily place them-

selves on the line, and then turn eyes to the front, without a particular command to that effect

321. Alignments to the rear will be executed on the same principles, the recruits stepping back a little beyond the line, and then dressing up according to the principles prescribed No. 312, the instructor commanding

Right (or left) backward—DRESS

322. After each alignment the instructor will examine the position of the men, and cause the rank to come to *ordered arms*, to prevent too much fatigue, and also the danger of negligence at *shouldered arms*

LESSON II.

323. The men having learned, in the first and second parts, to march with steadiness in common time, and to take steps equal in length and swiftness, will be exercised in the third part only in *quick time, double quick time,* and the *run;* the instructor will cause them to execute successively, at these different gaits, the march to the front, the facing about in marching, the march by the flank, the wheels at a halt and in marching, and the changes of direction to the side of the guides

324. The instructor will inform the recruits that at the command *march*, they will always move off in *quick time*, unless this command should be preceded by that of *double quick*

To march to the front

325. The rank being correctly aligned, when the instructor shall wish to cause it to march by the front, he will place a well instructed man on the right or the left, according to the side on which he may wish the guide to be, and command.

1. *Squad, forward.* 2. *Guide right (or left.)* 3. MARCH

326. At the command *march*, the rank will step off smartly with the left foot, the guide will take care to march straight to the front, keeping his shoulders always in a square with that line.

327. The instructor will observe, in marching to the front, that the men touch lightly the elbow towards the side of the guide, that they do not open out the left elbow nor the right arm; that they yield to pressure coming from the side of the guide, and resist that coming from the opposite side; that they recover by insensible degrees the slight touch of the elbow, if lost; that they maintain the head direct to the front, no matter on which side the guide may be, and if found before or behind the alignment, that the man in fault corrects himself by shortening or lengthening the step, by degrees, almost insensible

328. The instructor will labor to cause recruits to comprehend that the alignment can only be preserved, in marching, by the regularity of the step, the touch of the elbow, and the maintenance of the sh   if, for

example, the step of some be longer than that of others, or if some march faster than others, a separation of elbows, and a loss of the alignment, would be inevitable; that if (it being required that the head should be direct to the front) they do not strictly observe the touch of elbows, it would be impossible for an individual to judge whether he marches abreast with his neighbor, or not, and whether there be not an interval between them.

329. The impulsion of the quick step having a tendency to make men too easy and free in their movements, the instructor will be careful to regulate the cadence of this step, and to habituate them to preserve always the erectness of the body, and the due length of the pace

330 The men being well established in the principles of the direct march, the instructor will exercise them in marching obliquely The rank being in march, the instructor will command·

1. *Right (or left) oblique.* 2 MARCH

331 At the second command, each man will make a half face to the right (or left), and will then march straight forward in the new direction As the men no longer touch elbows, they will glance along the shoulders of the nearest files, towards the side to which they are obliquing, and will regulate their steps so that the shoulders shall always be behind that of their next neighbor on that side, and that his head shall conceal the heads of the other men in the rank Besides this, the men should preserve the same length of pace, and the same degree of obliquity

332 The instructor, wishing to resume the primitive direction, will command·

1 *Forward.* 2 MARCH

333 At the second command, each man will make a half face to the left (or right), and all will then march straight to the front, conforming to the principles of the direct march

To march to the front in double quick time

334 When the several principles, heretofore explained, have become familiar to the recruits, and they shall be well established in the position of the body, the bearing of arms, and the mechanism, length, and swiftness of the step, the instructor will pass them from *quick* to *double quick* time, and the reverse, observing not to make them march obliquely in double quick time, till they are well established in the cadence of this step.

335. The squad being at a march in quick time, the instructor will command:

1 *Double quick.* 2. MARCH

336 At the command *march*, which will be given when either foot is coming to the ground, the squad will step off in double quick time The men will endeavor to follow the principles laid down in the first part of this book, and to preserve the alignment.

337. When the instructor wishes the squad to resume the step in quick time, he will command.

1. *Quick time.* 2. MARCH.

338. At the command *march*, which will be given when either foot is coming to the ground, the squad will retake the step in quick time.

339. The squad being in march, the instructor will halt it by the commands and means prescribed Nos. 98 and 99. The command *halt*, will be given an instant before the foot is ready to be placed on the ground.

340. The squad being in march in double quick time, the instructor will occasionally cause it to mark time by the commands prescribed No. 240. The men will then mark double quick time, without altering the cadence of the step. He will also cause them to pass from the direct to the oblique step, and reciprocally, conforming to what has been prescribed No. 330, and following.

341. The squad being at a halt, the instructor will cause it to march in double quick time, by preceding the command *march*, by *double quick*.

342. The instructor will endeavor to regulate well the cadence of this step.

To face about in marching.

343. If the squad be marching in quick, or double quick time, and the instructor should wish to march it in retreat, he will command:

1. *Squad right about.* 2. MARCH.

344. At the command *march*, which will be given at the instant the left foot is coming to the ground, the recruit will bring this foot to the ground, and turning on it, will face to the rear; he will then place the right foot in the new direction, and step off with the left foot.

To march backwards.

345. The squad being at a halt, if the instructor should wish to march it in the back step, he will command:

1. *Squad backward.* 2. *Guide left* (or *right*). 3. MARCH.

346. The back step will be executed by the means prescribed No. 247.

347. The instructor, in this step, will be watchful that the men do not lean on each other.

348. As the march to the front in quick time should only be executed at shouldered arms, the instructor, in order not to fatigue the men too much, and also to prevent negligence in gait and position, will halt the squad from time to time, and cause arms to be ordered.

349. In marching at *double quick time*, the men will always carry their pieces on the right shoulder or at a trail. This rule is general.

350. If the instructor shall wish the pieces carried at a trail, he will give the command *trail arms*, before the command *double quick* If, on the contrary, this command be not given, the men will shift their pieces to the right shoulder at the command *double quick*. In either case, at the command *halt*, the men will bring their pieces to the position of *shoulder arms*. *This rule is general.*

LESSON III.—*The march by the flank.*

351. The rank being at a halt, and correctly aligned, the instructor will command

1. *Squad, right*—FACE 2. *Forward.* 3 MARCH.

352. At the last part of the first command, the rank will face to the right; the even numbered men, after facing to the right, will step quickly to the right side of the odd numbered men, the latter standing fast, so that when the movement is executed, the men will be formed into files of two men abreast.

353 At the third command, the squad will step off smartly with the left foot, the files keeping aligned, and preserving their intervals

354 The march by the left flank will be executed by the same commands, substituting the word *left* for *right*, and by inverse means, in this case, the even numbered men, after facing to the left, will stand fast, and the odd numbered will place themselves on their left.

355 The instructor will place a well-instructed soldier by the side of the recruit who is at the head of the rank, to regulate the step, and to conduct him, and it will be enjoined on this recruit to march always elbow to elbow with the soldier.

356 The instructor will cause to be observed in the march, by the flank, the following rules

That the step be executed according to the principles prescribed for the direct step;

Because these principles, without which men, placed elbow to elbow, in the same rank, cannot preserve unity and harmony of movement, are of a more necessary observance in marching in file

That the head of the man who immediately precedes, covers the heads of all who are in front,

Because it is the most certain rule by which each man may maintain himself in the exact line of the file

357 The instructor will place himself habitually five or six paces on the flank of the rank marching in file, to watch over the execution of the principles prescribed above He will also place himself sometimes in its rear, halt, and suffer it to pass fifteen or twenty paces, the better to see whether the men cover each other accurately.

358 When he shall wish to halt the rank, marching by the flank, and to cause it to face to the front, he will command.

1 *Squad* 2 Halt 3 Front

359. At the second command, the rank will halt, and afterwards no man will stir, although he may have lost his distance. This prohibition is necessary, to habituate the men to a constant preservation of their distances.

360. At the third command, each man will front by facing to the left, if marching by the right flank, and by a face to the right, if marching by the left flank. The rear rank men will at the same time move quickly into their places, so as to form the squad again into one rank.

361. When the men have become accustomed to marching by the flank, the instructor will cause them to change direction by file; for this purpose, he will command.

1 *By file left* (or *right*) 2 March

362. At the command *march*, the first file will change direction to the left (or right) in describing a small arc of a circle, and will then march straight forward; the two men of this file, in wheeling, will keep up the touch of the elbows, and the man on the side to which the wheel is made, will shorten the first three or four steps. Each file will come successively to wheel on the same spot where that which preceded it wheeled.

363. The instructor will also cause the squad to face by the right or left flank in marching, and for this purpose will command:

1 *Squad by the right* (or *left*) *flank* 2 March

364. At the second command, which will be given a little before either foot comes to the ground, the recruits will turn the body, plant the foot that is raised in the new direction, and step off with the other foot without altering the cadence of the step, the men will double or undouble rapidly.

365. If, in facing by the right or left flank, the squad should face to the rear, the men will come into one rank, agreeably to the principles indicated No 360. It is to be remarked that it is the men who are in rear who always move up to form into single rank and in such manner as never to invert the order of the numbers in the rank

366. If, when the squad has been faced to the rear, the instructor should cause it to face by the left flank, it is the even numbers who will double by moving to the left of the odd numbers; but if by the right flank, it is the odd numbers who will double to the right of the even numbers.

367. This lesson, like the preceding one, will be practiced with pieces at a shoulder, but the instructor may, to give relief by change, occasionally order *support arms*, and he will require of the recruits marching in this position, as much regularity as in the former

The march by the flank in double quick time.

368. The principles of the march by the flank in double quick

time, are the same as in quick time. The instructor will give the commands prescribed No. 351, taking care always to give the command *double quick* before that of *march*.

369. He will pay the greatest attention to the cadence of the step.

370. The instructor will cause the change of direction, and the march by the flank, to be executed in double quick time, by the same commands, and according to the same principles as in quick time.

371. The instructor will cause the pieces to be carried either on the *right shoulder* or at a *trail*.

372. The instructor will sometimes march the squad by the flank, without doubling the files.

373. The principles of this march are the same as in two ranks, and it will always be executed in quick time.

374. The instructor will give the commands prescribed No. 351, but he will be careful to caution the squad not to double files.

375. The instructor will be watchful that the men do not bend their knees unequally, which would cause them to tread on the heels of the men in front, and also to lose the cadence of the step and their distances.

376. The various movements in this lesson will be executed in single rank. In the changes of direction, the leading man will change direction without altering the length or the cadence of the step. The instructor will recall to the attention of the men, that in facing by the right or left flank in marching, they will not double, but march in one rank.

LESSON IV.—WHEELINGS.—*General principles of Wheelings.*

377. Wheelings are of two kinds: from halts, or on fixed pivots, and in march or on moveable pivots.

378. Wheeling on a fixed pivot takes place in passing a corps from the order in battle to the order in column, or from the latter to the former.

379. Wheels in marching take place in changes of direction in column, as often as this movement is executed to the side opposite to the guide.

380. In wheels from a halt, the pivot-man only turns in his place, without advancing or receding.

381. In the wheels in marching, the pivot takes steps of nine or eleven inches, according as the squad is marching in quick or double quick time, so as to clear the wheeling point, which is necessary, in order that the subdivisions of a column may change direction without losing their distances, as will be explained in the school of the company.

382. The man on the wheeling flank will take the full step of twenty-eight inches, or thirty-three inches, according to the gait.

Wheeling from a halt, or on a fixed pivot.

383. The rank being at a halt, the instructor will place a well-

instructed man on the wheeling flank to conduct it, and then command

1 *By squad, right wheel.* 2. MARCH

384 At the second command, the rank will step off with the left foot, turning at the same time the head a little to the left, the eyes fixed on the line of the eyes of the men to their left, the pivot-man will merely mark time in gradually turning his body, in order to conform himself to the movement of the marching flank; the man who conducts this flank will take steps of twenty-eight inches, and from the first step advance a little the left shoulder, cast his eyes from time to time along the rank and feel constantly the elbow of the next man lightly, but never push him

385 The other man will feel lightly the elbow of the next man towards the pivot, resist pressure coming from the opposite side, and each will conform himself to the marching flank—shortening his step according to his approximation to the pivot

386. The instructor will make the rank wheel round the circle once or twice before halting, in order to cause the principles to be the better understood, and he will be watchful that the center does not break.

387. He will cause the wheel to the left to be executed according to the same principles

388 When the instructor shall wish to arrest the wheel, he will command:

1. *Squad.* 2. HALT.

389 At the second command, the rank will halt, and no man stir. The instructor, going to the flank opposite the pivot, will place the two outer men of that flank in the direction he may wish to give to the rank, without however displacing the pivot, who will conform the line of his shoulders to this direction. The instructor will take care to have between these two men, and the pivot, only the space necessary to contain the other men. He will then command.

Left (or *right*)—DRESS

390 At this, the rank will place itself on the alignment of the two men established as the basis, in conformity with the principles prescribed.

391. The instructor will next command FRONT, which will be executed as prescribed No 314

Remarks on the principles of the wheel from a halt

392. *Turn a little the head towards the marching flank, and fix the eyes on the line of the eyes of the men who are on that side;*

Because, otherwise, it would be impossible for each man to regulate the length of his step so as to conform his own movement to that of the marching flank.

Touch lightly the elbow of the next man towards the pivot;

In order that the files may not open out in the wheel

Resist pressure that comes from the side of the marching flank,

Because, if this principle be neglected, the pivot, which ought to be a fixed point, in wheels from a halt, might be pushed out of its place by pressure.

Wheeling in marching, or on a movable pivot.

393 When the recruits have been taught to execute well the wheel from a halt, they will be taught to wheel in marching.

394 To this end, the rank being in march, when the instructor shall wish to cause it to change direction to the reverse flank, (to the side opposite to the guide or pivot flank,) he will command:

1 *Right* (or *left*) *wheel.* 2 MARCH

395. The first command will be given when the rank is yet *four* paces from the wheeling point

396 At the second command, the wheel will be executed in the same manner as from a halt, except that the touch of the elbow will remain towards the marching flank (or side of the guide) instead of the side of the actual pivot, that the pivot man, instead of merely turning in his place, will conform himself to the movement of the marching flank, feel lightly the elbow of the next man, take steps of full nine inches, and thus gain ground forward in describing a small curve so as to clear the point of the wheel The middle of the rank will bend slightly to the rear As soon as the movement shall commence, the man who conducts the marching flank will cast his eyes on the ground over which he will have to pass

397 The wheel being ended, the instructor will command:

1 *Forward.* 2. MARCH

398 The first command will be pronounced when *four* paces are yet required to complete the change of direction

399 At the command *march*, which will be given at the instant of completing the wheel, the man who conducts the marching flank will direct himself straight forward, the pivot-man and all the rank will retake the step of twenty-eight inches, and bring the head direct to the front.

Turning. or change of direction to the side of the guide.

400 The change of direction to the side of the guide, in marching, will be executed as follows The instructor will command:

1. *Left* (or *right*) *turn.* 2. MARCH

401 The first command will be given when the rank is yet *four* paces from the turning point

402 At the command *march*, to be pronounced at the instant the rank ought to turn, the guide will face to the left (or right) in marching, and move forward in the new direction without slackening or quickening the cadence, and without shortening or lengthening the step The whole rank will promptly conform

itself to the new direction, to effect which, each man will advance the shoulder opposite to the guide, take the double quick step, to carry himself in the new direction, turn the head and eyes to the side of the guide, and retake the touch of the elbow on that side, in placing himself on the alignment of the guide, from whom he will take the step, and then resume the direct position of the head. Each man will thus arrive successively on the alignment.

Wheeling and changing direction to the side of the guide, in double quick time.

403. When the recruits comprehend and execute well, in quick time, the wheels at a halt and in marching, and the change of direction to the side of the guide, the instructor will cause the same movements to be repeated in double quick time.

404. These various movements will be executed by the same commands and according to the same principles as in quick time, except that the command *double quick* will precede that of *march*. In wheeling while marching, the pivot man will take steps of eleven inches, and in the changes of direction to the side of the guide, the men on the side opposite the guide must increase the gait in order to bring themselves into line.

405. The instructor, in order not to fatigue the recruits, and not to divide their attention, will cause them to execute the several movements of which this lesson is composed first without arms, and next, after the mechanism be well comprehended, with arms.

LESSON V.—*Long marches in double quick time and the run.*

406. The instructor will cause to be resumed the exercises in double quick time and the run, with arms and knapsacks.

407. He will cause long marches to be executed in double quick time, both by the front and by the flank, and by constant practice will lead the men to pass over a distance of five miles in sixty minutes. The pieces will be carried on either shoulder, and sometimes at a trail.

408. He will also exercise them in long marches at a run, the pieces carried at will; the men will be instructed to keep as united as possible, without however exacting much regularity, which is impracticable.

409. The run, in actual service, will only be resorted to when it may be highly important to reach a given point with great promptitude.

To stack arms.

The men being at order arms, the instructor will command

*Stack—*ARMS.

410. At this command the front rank man of every even numbered file will pass his piece before him, seizing it with the left hand near the upper band; will place the butt a little in advance of his left toe, the barrel turned towards the body, and draw the rammer... the front rank man of every odd

numbered file will also draw the rammer slightly, and pass his piece to the man next on his left, who will seize it with the right hand near the upper band, and place the butt a little in advance of the right toe of the man next on his right, the barrel turned to the front, he will then cross the rammers of the two pieces, the rammer of the piece of the odd numbered man being inside; the rear rank man of every even file will also draw his rammer, lean his piece forward, the lock plate downwards, advance the right foot about six inches, and insert the rammer between the rammer and barrel of the piece of his front rank man, with his left hand he will place the butt of his piece on the ground, thirty-two inches in rear of, and perpendicular to, the front rank, bringing back his right foot by the side of the left; the front rank man of every even file will at the same time lean the stack to the rear, quit it with his right hand and force all the rammers down. The stack being thus formed, the rear rank man of every odd file will pass his piece into his left hand, the barrel to the front, and inclining it forward, will rest it on the stack.

411. The men of both ranks having taken the position of the soldier without arms, the instructor will command

1 *Break ranks* 2 March

To resume arms

412. Both ranks being re-formed in rear of their stacks, the instructor will command

Take—Arms

413. At this command the rear rank man of every odd numbered file will withdraw his piece from the stack; the front rank man of every even file will seize his own piece with the left hand and that of the man on his right with his right hand, both above the lower band, the rear rank man of the even file will seize his piece with the right hand below the lower band; these two men will raise up the stack to loosen the rammers, the front rank man of every odd file will facilitate the disengagement of the rammers, if necessary, by drawing them out slightly with the left hand, and will receive his piece from the hand of the man next on his left; the four men will retake the position of the soldier at order arms.

END OF THE SCHOOL OF THE SOLDIER.

TITLE THIRD

SCHOOL OF THE COMPANY.

General Rules and Division of the School of the Company

1. Instruction by company will always precede that by battalion, and the object being to prepare the soldiers for the higher school, the exercises of detail by company will be strictly adhered to, as well in respect to principles, as the order of progression herein prescribed.

2. There will be attached to a company undergoing elementary instruction, a captain, a covering sergeant, and a certain number of file closers, the whole posted in the manner indicated, Title First, and, according to the same Title, the officer charged with the exercise of such company will herein be denominated the *instructor*.

3. The School of the Company will be divided into six lessons, and each lesson will comprehend five articles, as follows:

LESSON I

1. To open ranks.
2. Alignments in open ranks.
3. Manual of arms.
4. To close ranks.
5. Alignments, and manual of arms in closed ranks.

LESSON II

1. To load in four times and at will.
2. To fire by company.
3. To fire by file.
4. To fire by rank.
5. To fire by the rear rank.

LESSON III.

1. To march in line of battle.
2. To halt the company marching in line of battle, and to allign it.
3. Oblique march in line of battle.
4. To mark time, to march in double quick time, and the back step.
5. To march in retreat in line of battle.

LESSON IV.

1. To march by the flank.
2. To change direction by file.
3. To halt the company marching by the flank, and to face it to the front.

4. The company being in march by the flank, to form it on the right or left by file into line of battle

5. The company marching by the flank, to form it by company or platoon into line, and cause it to face to the right and left in marching

LESSON V

1. To break into column by platoon either at a halt or while marching.
2. To march in column
3. To change direction
4. To halt the column
5. Being in column by platoon, to form to the right or left into line of battle, either at a halt or marching

LESSON VI

1. To break into platoons, and to re-form the company
2. To break files to the rear, and to cause them to re-enter into line
3. To march in column *in route*, and to execute the movements incident thereto
4. Countermarch
5. Being in column by platoon, to form on the right or left into line of battle

4. The company will always be formed in two ranks. The instructor will then cause the files to be numbered, and for this purpose will command:

In each rank—Count Twos

5. At this command, the men count in each rank, from right to left, pronouncing in a loud and distinct voice, in the same tone, without hurry and without turning the head, *one, two*, according to the place which each one occupies. He will also cause the company to be divided into platoons and sections, taking care that the first platoon is always composed of an even number of files

6. The instructor will be as clear and concise as possible in his explanations; he will cause faults of detail to be rectified by the captain, to whom he will indicate them, if the captain should not have himself observed them; and the instructor will not otherwise interfere, unless the captain should not well comprehend, or should badly execute his intentions

7. Composure, or presence of mind, in him who commands, and in those who obey, being the first means of order in a body of troops, the instructor will labor to habituate the company to this essential quality, and will himself give the example

LESSON FIRST

ARTICLE FIRST—*To open ranks*

8. The company being at ordered arms, the rank and file closers well aligned, when the instructor shall wish to cause the ranks to

be opened, he will direct the left guide to place himself on the left of the front rank, which being executed, he will command

1. *Attention.* 2. *Company.* 3. *Shoulder*—ARMS. 4. *To the rear open order*

9. At the fourth command, the covering sergeant, and the left guide, will step off smartly to the rear, four paces from the front rank, in order to mark the alignment of the rear rank. They will judge this distance by the eye, without counting the steps.

10. The instructor will place himself at the same time on the right flank, in order to observe, if these two non-commissioned officers are on a line parallel to the front rank, and if necessary, to correct their positions, which being executed, he will command

5. MARCH.

11. At this command, the front rank will stand fast.

12. The rear rank will step to the rear, without counting the steps, and will place themselves on the alignment marked for this rank, conforming to what is prescribed in the school of the soldier, No. 321.

13. The covering sergeant will align the rear rank on the left guide placed to mark the left of this rank.

14. The file closers will march to the rear at the same time with the rear rank, and will place themselves two paces from this rank when it is aligned.

15. The instructor seeing the rear rank aligned, will command.

6. FRONT.

16. At this command, the sergeant on the left of the rear rank will return to his place as a file closer.

17. The rear rank being aligned, the instructor will direct the captain and the covering sergeant to observe the men in their respective ranks, and to correct, if necessary, the positions of persons and pieces.

ARTICLE SECOND —*Alignments in open ranks*

18. The ranks being open, the instructor will, in the first exercises, align the ranks, man by man, the better to inculcate the principles.

19. To effect this, he will cause two or four men on the right or left of each rank to march two or three paces forward, and, after having aligned them, command

By file right (or *left*)—DRESS

20. At this, the men of each rank will move up successively on the alignment, each man being preceded by his neighbor in the same rank, towards the basis, by two paces, and having correctly aligned himself

dress correctly, the instructor will cause the ranks to align themselves at once, forward and backward, sometimes in a direction parallel, and sometimes in one oblique, to the original direction, giving, in each case, two or four men to serve as a basis of alignment to each rank. To effect which, he will command:

1. *Right* (or *left*)—Dress. 2. Front.

Or,

1. *Right* (or *left*) *backward*—Dress. 2. Front.

22. In oblique alignments, in *opened* ranks, the men of the rear rank will not seek to cover their file leaders, as the sole object of the exercise is to teach them to align themselves correctly in their respective ranks, in the different directions.

23. In the several alignments, the captain will superintend the front rank, and the covering sergeant the rear rank. For this purpose, they will place themselves on the side by which the ranks are dressed.

24. In oblique alignments, the men will conform the line of their shoulders to the new direction of their rank, and will place themselves on the alignment as has been prescribed in the School of the Soldier, No. 317 or No. 321, according as the new direction shall be in front or rear of the original one.

25. At the end of each alignment, the captain and the covering sergeant will pass along the front of the ranks to correct the positions of persons and arms.

Article Third.—*Manual of arms.*

26. The ranks being open, the instructor will place himself in a position to see the ranks, and will command the manual of arms in the following order:

Present arms. (then) *Shoulder arms.*
Order arms
Ground arms
Raise arms   *Shoulder arms*
Support arms   *Shoulder arms*
Fix bayonet   *Shoulder arms*
Charge bayonet   *Shoulder arms*
Trail arms   *Shoulder arms*
Unfix bayonet   *Shoulder arms*
Secure arms   *Shoulder arms*
Load in nine times

27. The instructor will take care that the position of the body, of the feet, and of the piece, be always exact, and that the times be briskly executed and close to the person.

Article Fourth.—*To close ranks.*

28. The manual of arms being ended, the instructor will command:

SCHOOL OF THE COMPANY.

1 *Close order.* 2 MARCH.

29. At the command *march*, the rear rank will close up in quick time, each man directing himself on his file leader.

ARTICLE V.—*Alignments, and manual of arms in closed ranks.*

30. The ranks being closed, the instructor will cause to be executed parallel and oblique alignments by the right and left, forward and backward, observing to place always two or four files to serve as a basis of alignment. He will give the commands prescribed, No. 21.

31. In alignments in closed ranks, the captain will superintend the front rank, and the covering sergeant the rear rank. They will habituate themselves to judge the alignment by the lines of the eyes and shoulders, in casting a glance of the eye along the front and rear of the ranks.

32. The moment the captain perceives the greater number of the front rank aligned, he will command FRONT, and rectify, afterwards, if necessary, the alignment of the other men by the means prescribed in the School of the Soldier, No 320. The rear rank will conform to the alignment of the front rank, superintended by the covering sergeant.

33. The ranks being steady, the instructor will place himself on the flank to verify their alignment. He will also see that each rear rank man covers accurately his file leader.

34. In oblique alignments, the instructor will observe what is prescribed No 24.

35. In all alignments, the file closers will preserve the distance of two paces from the rear rank.

36. The alignments being ended, the instructor will cause to be executed the manual of arms.

37. The instructor, wishing to rest the men, without deranging the alignment, will first cause arms to be supported, or ordered, and then command

In place—REST.

38. At this command, the men will no longer be constrained to preserve silence or steadiness of position, but they will always keep one or other heel on the alignment.

39. If, on the contrary, the instructor should wish to rest the men without constraining them to preserve the alignment, he will command.

REST.

40. At which command, the men will not be required to preserve immobility, or to remain in their places.

41. the instructor may, also, when he shall judge proper, cause arms to be stacked, which will be executed as prescribed, school of the soldier.

LESSON II

42. The instructor, wishing to pass to the second lesson, will

cause the company to take arms, if stacks have been formed, and command

    1. *Attention* 2. *Company* 3 *Shoulder*—ARMS

43 The instructor will then cause loadings and firings to be executed in the following order:

ARTICLE I —*To load at four times and at will*

44. Loading in four *times* will be commanded and executed as prescribed in the school of the soldier, No. 251, and following. The instructor will cause this exercise to be often repeated, in succession, before passing to load at will

45. Loading at will will be commanded and executed as prescribed in the school for the soldier, No. 256 In priming when loading in four *times*, and also at will, the captain and covering sergeant will half face to the right with the men, and face to the front when the man next to them, respectively, brings his piece to the shoulder

46 The instructor will labor to the utmost to cause the men, in the different loadings, to execute what has been prescribed in the school of the soldier, Nos 257 and 258

47 Loading at will, being that of battle, and consequently the one with which it is most important to render the men familiar, it will claim preference in the exercises the moment the men be well established in the principles. To these they will be brought by degrees, so that every man may be able to load with cartridges and to fire at least three rounds in a minute with ease and regularity

ARTICLE II —*To fire by Company*

48. The instructor, wishing to cause the fire by company to be executed, will command

    1 *Fire by Company* 2 *Commence firing*

49 At the first command, the captain will promptly place himself opposite the center of his company, and four paces in rear of the line of file closers: the covering sergeant will retire to that line, and place himself opposite to his interval *This rule is general, for both the captain and covering sergeant, in all the different firings*

50 At the second command, the captain will add. 1. *Company*, 2 READY, 3 AIM, 4 FIRE, 5 LOAD

51. At the command *load*, the men will load their pieces, and then take the position *ready*, as prescribed in the school of the soldier.

52. The captain will immediately recommence the firing, by the commands

    1. *Company* 2. AIM 3 FIRE. 4 LOAD.

53 The firing will be thus continued until the signal to cease firing is sounded.

54. The captain will sometimes cause aim to be taken to the right and left, simply observing to pronounce *right* (or *left*) *oblique*, before the command *aim*

ARTICLE III.—*The fire by file*

55. The instructor wishing to cause the fire by file to be executed, will command

1 *Fire by file* 2 *Company.* 3 READY. 4 *Commence firing.*

56. The third and fourth commands will be executed as prescribed in the school of the soldier, No. 275 and following

57. The fire will be commenced by the right file of the company, the next file will take aim at the instant the first brings down pieces to re-load, and so on to the left, but this progression will only be observed in the first discharge, after which each man will re-load and fire without regulating himself by others, conforming himself to what is prescribed in the school of the soldier, No 280

ARTICLE IV.—*The fire by rank*

58. The instructor wishing the fire by rank to be executed, will command

1. *Fire by rank.* 2 *Company* 3. READY 4 *Rear Rank*—AIM.
   5 FIRE. 6. LOAD

59. The fifth and sixth commands will be executed as is prescribed in the school of the soldier, No 285 and following

60. When the instructor sees one or two pieces in the rear rank at a ready, he will command

1 *Front Rank* 2 AIM 3. FIRE. 4. LOAD

61. The firing will be continued thus by alternate ranks, until the signal is given to cease firing.

62. The instructor will sometimes cause aim to be taken to the right and left, conforming to what is prescribed No 54.

63. The instructor will cause the firing to cease, whether by company, by file, or by rank, by sounding the signal to cease firing, and at the instant this sound commences, the men will cease to fire, conforming to what is prescribed in the school of the soldier, No. 282.

64. The signal to cease firing will always be followed by a bugle note; at which sound, the captain and covering sergeant will promptly resume their places in line, and will rectify, if necessary, the alignment of the ranks.

65. In this school, except when powder is used, the signal to cease firing will be indicated by the command *cease firing*, which will be pronounced by the instructor when he wishes the semblance of firing to cease

66. The command *posts* will be likewise substituted, under similar circumstances, for the bugle note employed as the signal for the return of the captain and covering sergeant to their places in

line, which command will be given when the instructor sees the men have brought their pieces to a shoulder

67. The fire by file being that which is most frequently used against an enemy, it is highly important that it be rendered perfectly familiar to the troops. The instructor will, therefore, give it almost exclusive preference, and labor to cause the men to aim with care, and always, if possible, at some particular object. As it is of the utmost importance that the men should aim with precision in battle, this principle will be rigidly enforced in the exercises for the purposes of instruction.

ARTICLE V.— *To Fire by the rear rank*

68. The instructor will cause the several fires to be executed to the rear, that is, by the rear rank. To effect this, he will command.

1. *Face by the rear rank.* 2. *Company.* 3. *About*—FACE

69. At the first command, the captain will step out and place himself near to, and facing the right file of his company, the covering sergeant, and file closers, will pass quickly through the captain's interval, and place themselves faced to the rear, the covering sergeant a pace behind the captain, and the file closers two paces from the front rank opposite to their places in line, each passing behind the covering sergeant

70. At the third command, which will be given at the instant the last file closer shall have passed through the interval, the company will face about; the captain will place himself in his interval in the rear rank, now become the front, and the covering sergeant will cover him in the front rank, now become the rear

71. The company having faced by the rear rank, the instructor will cause it to execute the fire by company, both direct and oblique, the fire by file, and the fire by rank, by the commands and means prescribed in the three preceding articles; the captain, covering sergeant, and the men will conform themselves, in like manner, to what is therein prescribed

72. The fire by file will commence on the left of the company, now become the right. In the fire by rank, the firing will commence with the front rank, now become the rear.

73. To resume the proper front, the instructor will command

1. *Face by the front rank* 2. *Company.* 3. *About*—FACE.

74. At the first command, the captain covering sergeant and file closers will conform to what is prescribed Nos 60 and 70

75. At the third command, the company having faced about, the captain and covering sergeant will resume their places in line.

76. In this lesson, the instructor will impress on the men the importance of aiming always at some particular object, and of holding the piece as prescribed in the school of the soldier, No. 178.

77. The instructor will recommend to the captain to make a

short pause between the commands *aim* and *fire*, to give the men time to aim with accuracy

78. The instructor will place himself in position to see the two ranks, in order to detect faults, he will charge the captain and file closers to be equally watchful, and to report to him when the ranks are at rest. He will remand, for individual instruction, the men who may be observed to load badly.

79. The instructor will recommend to the soldiers, in the firings, the highest degree of composure or presence of mind, he will neglect nothing that may contribute to this end

80. He will give to the men, *as a general principle*, to maintain, in the direct fire, the left heel in its place, in order that the alignment of the ranks and files may not be deranged; and he will verify, by examination, after each exercise in firing, the observance of this principle.

81. The instructor will observe, in addition to these remarks, all those which follow

82. When the firing is executed with cartridges, it is particularly recommended that the men observe, in uncocking, whether smoke escapes from the tube, which is a certain indication that the piece has been discharged; but if, on the contrary, no smoke escapes, the soldier, in such case, instead of reloading, will pick and prime again. If, believing the load to be discharged, the soldier should put a second cartridge in his piece, he ought, at least, to perceive it in ramming, by the hight of the load; and he would be very culpable should he put in a third. The instructor will always cause arms to be inspected after firing with cartridges, in order to observe if the fault has been committed, of putting three cartridges, without a discharge, in the same piece, in which case the ball screw will be applied

83. It sometimes happens when a cap has missed fire, that the tube is found stopped up with a hard, white, and compact powder; in this case, picking will be dispensed with, and a new cap substituted for the old one.

LESSON THIRD.

ARTICLE I.—*To advance in line of battle.*

84. The company being in line of battle, and correctly aligned, when the instructor shall wish to exercise it in marching by the front, he will assure himself that the shoulders of the captain and covering sergeant are perfectly in the direction of their respective ranks, and that the sergeant accurately covers the captain; the instructor will then place himself twenty-five or thirty paces in front of them, face to the rear, and place himself exactly on the prolongation of the line passing between their heels.

85. The instructor, being aligned on the directing file, will command:

*, 1. *Company, forward.*

86. At the

paces in advance of the captain the instructor, from the position prescribed, will correctly align this sergeant on the prolongation of the directing file.

87. This advanced sergeant, who is to be charged with the direction, will, the moment his position is assured, take two points on the ground in the straight line which would pass between his own and the heels of the instructor

88. These dispositions being made, the instructor will step aside, and command:

2. March.

89. At this, the company will step off with life The directing sergeant will observe, with the greatest precision, the length and cadence of the step, marching on the two points he has chosen, he will take in succession, and always a little before arriving at the point nearest to him, new points in advance, exactly in the same line with the first two, and at the distance of some fifteen or twenty paces from each other. The captain will march steadily in the trace of the directing sergeant, keeping always six paces from him; the men will each maintain the head direct to the front, feel lightly the elbow of his neighbor on the side of direction, and conform himself to the principles, school of the soldier, for the march by front

90. The man next to the captain will take special care not to pass him, to this end, he will keep the line of his shoulders a little in the rear, but in the same direction with those of the captain

91. The file closers will march at the habitual distance of two paces behind the rear rank

92 If the men lose the step, the instructor will command

To the—Step.

93. At this command, the men will glance towards the directing sergeant, retake the step from him, and again direct their eyes to the front.

94 The instructor will cause the captain and covering sergeant to be posted sometimes on the right, and sometimes on the left of the company

95. The directing sergeant, in advance, having the greatest influence on the march of the company, he will be selected for the precision of his step, his habit of maintaining his shoulders in a square with a given line of direction, and of prolonging that line without variation.

96 If this sergeant should fail to observe these principles, undulations in the front of the company must necessarily follow, the men will be unable to contract the habit of taking steps equal in length and swiftness, and of maintaining their shoulders in a square with the line of direction—the only means of attaining perfection in the march in line.

97. The instructor, with a view the better to establish the men in the length and cadence of the step, and in the principles of the

march in line, will cause the company to advance three or four hundred paces, at once, without halting, if the ground will permit. In the first exercises, he will march the company with open ranks, the better to observe the two ranks.

98. The instructor will see, with care, that all the principles of the march in line are strictly observed; he will generally be on the directing flank, in a position to observe the two ranks, and the faults they may commit; he will sometimes halt behind the directing file during some thirty successive steps, in order to judge whether the directing sergeant, or the directing file, deviate from the perpendicular.

ARTICLE II.—*To halt the company, marching in line of battle, and to align it.*

99. The instructor, wishing to halt the company, will command

1. *Company.* 2. HALT.

100. At the second command, the company will halt, the directing sergeant will remain in advance, unless ordered to return to the line of file closers. The company being at a halt, the instructor may advance the first three or four files on the side of direction, and align the company on that basis, or he may confine himself to causing the alignment to be rectified. In this last case, he will command *Captain, rectify the alignment.* The captain will direct the covering sergeant to attend to the rear rank, when each, glancing his eyes along his rank, will promptly rectify it, conforming to what is prescribed in the school of the soldier, No. 320.

ARTICLE III.—*Oblique march in line of battle.*

101. The company being in the direct march, when the instructor shall wish to cause it to march obliquely, he will command

1. *Right* (or *left*) *oblique.* 2. MARCH.

102. At the command *march*, the company will take the oblique step. The men will accurately observe the principles prescribed in the school of the soldier, No. 231. The rear rank men will preserve their distances, and march in rear of the man next on the right (or left) of their habitual file leaders.

103. When the instructor wishes the direct march to be resumed, he will command:

1. *Forward.* 2. MARCH.

104. At the command *march*, the company will resume the direct march. The instructor will move briskly twenty paces in front of the captain, and facing the company, will place himself exactly in the prolongation of the captain and covering sergeant; and then, by a sign, will move the directing sergeant on the same line, if he be not already on it; the latter will immediately take two points on the ground between himself and the instructor, and as he advances, will take new points as prescribed No. 89.

105. In the oblique march, the men not having the touch of elbows, the guide will aways be on the side toward which the oblique is made, without any indication to that effect being given, and when the direct march is resumed, the guide will be, equally without indication, on the side where it was previous to the oblique

106. The instructor will, at first, cause the oblique to be made toward the side of the guide. He will also direct the captain to have an eye on the directing sergeant, in order to keep on the same perpendicular line to the front with him, while following a parallel direction.

107. During the continuance of the march, the instructor will be watchful that the men follow parallel directions, in conforming to the principles prescribed in the school of the soldier, for preserving the general alignment, whenever the men lose the alignment, he will be careful that they regain it by lengthening or shortening the step, without altering the cadence, or changing the direction.

108 The instructor will place himself in front of the company and face to it, in order to regulate the march of the directing sergeant, or the man who is on the flank toward which the oblique is made, and to see that the principles of the march are properly observed, and that the files do not crowd.

ARTICLE IV.—*To mark time, to march in double quick time, and the back step*

109 The company being in the direct march, and in quick time, the instructor, to cause it to mark time, will command.

    1 *Mark time*   2 MARCH.

110. To resume the march, he will command

    1 *Forward*   2 MARCH.

111 To cause the march in double quick time, the instructor will command

    1 *'Double quick*   2 MARCH

112. The command *march* will be pronounced at the instant either foot is coming to the ground

113 To resume quick time, the instructor will command:

    1. *Quick time*   2 MARCH.

114 The command *march* will be pronounced at the instant either foot is coming to the ground

115 The company being at a halt, the instructor may cause it to march in the back step, to this effect, he will command

    1 *Company backward*   2 MARCH.

116. The back step will be executed according to the principles prescribed in the school of the soldier, No. 247, but the use of it being rare, the instructor will not cause more than fifteen or twenty steps to be taken in succession, and to that extent but seldom.

117. The instructor ought not to exercise the company in march-

ing in double quick time till the men are well established in the length and swiftness of the pace in quick time, he will then endeavor to render the march of one hundred and sixty-five steps in the minute equally easy and familiar, and also cause them to observe the same erectness of body and composure of mind, as if marching in quick time

118. When marching in double quick time, if a subdivision (in a column) has to change direction by *turning*, or has to form into line, the men will quicken the pace to one hundred and eighty steps in a minute. The same swiftness of step will be observed under all circumstances where great rapidity of movement is required. But, as ranks of men cannot march any length of time at so swift a rate, without breaking or confusion, this acceleration will not be considered a prescribed exercise, and accordingly companies or battalions will only be habitually exercised in the double quick time of one hundred and sixty-five steps in the minute.

ARTICLE V — *To march in retreat.*

119. The company being halted and correctly aligned, when the instructor shall wish to cause it to march in retreat, he will command

1. *Company.* 2. *About*—FACE.

120. The company having faced to the rear, the instructor will place himself in front of the directing file, conforming to what is prescribed, No 84

121. The instructor, being correctly established on the prolongation of the directing file, will command

3. *Company, forward*

122 At this, the directing sergeant will conform himself to what is prescribed Nos. 86 and 87, with this difference—he will place himself six paces in front of the line of file closers, now leading.

123 The covering sergeant will step into the line of file closers, opposite to his interval, and the captain will place himself in the rear rank, now become the front

124. This disposition being promptly made, the instructor will command:

4. MARCH

125 At this, the directing sergeant, the captain, and the men, will conform themselves to what is prescribed No 89, and following.

126 The instructor will cause to be executed, marching in retreat, all that is prescribed for marching in advance, the commands and the means of execution will be the same.

127 The instructor having halted the company, will, when he may wish, cause it to face to the front by the commands prescribed No. 119. The captain, the covering sergeant, and the directing sergeant, will resume their habitual places in line, the moment they shall have faced about

128. The company being on a march in retreat, the in-

structor should wish to march in retreat, he will cause the right about to be executed while marching, and to this effect will command

   1 *Company.* 2 *Right about.* 3. MARCH

129. At the third command, the company will promptly face about, and recommence the march by the rear rank

130. The directing sergeant will face about with the company, and will move rapidly six paces in front of the file closers, and upon the prolongation of the guide. The instructor will place him in the proper direction by the means prescribed No. 104. The captain, the covering sergeant, and the men, will conform to the principles prescribed for the march in retreat

131. When the instructor wishes the company to march by the front rank, he will give the same commands, and will regulate the direction of the march by the same means.

132. The instructor will cause to be executed in double quick time, all the movements prescribed in the 3d, 4th, 5th and 6th lessons of this school, with the exception of the march backwards, which will be executed only in quick time. He will give the same commands, observing to add *double quick* before the command *march.*

133. When the pieces are carried on the right shoulder, in quick time, the distance between the ranks will be sixteen inches. Whenever, therefore, the instructor brings the company from a shoulder to this position, the rear rank must shorten a little the first steps in order to gain the prescribed distance, and will lengthen the steps, on the contrary, in order to close up when the pieces are again brought to a shoulder. In marching in double quick time he distance between the ranks will be twenty-six inches, and the pieces will be carried habitually on the right shoulder.

134. Whenever a company is halted, the men will bring their pieces at once to a shoulder at the command *halt.* The rear rank will close to its proper distance. *These rules are general.*

SCHOOL OF THE COMPANY.

LESSON FOURTH.

ARTICLE 1.—*To march by the flank.*

135. The company being in line of battle, and at a halt, when the instructor shall wish to cause it to march by the right flank, he will command:

1. *Company, right*—FACE. 2. *Forward.* 3. MARCH.

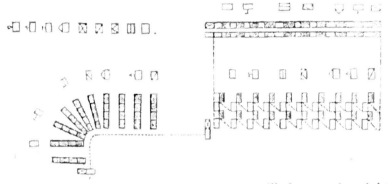

136. At the first command, the company will face to the right, the covering sergeant will place himself at the head of the front rank, the captain having stepped out for the purpose, so far as to find himself by the side of the sergeant, and on his left; the front rank will double as is prescribed in the school of the soldier, No. 352; the rear rank will, at the same time, side step to the right one pace, and double in the same manner; so that when the movement is completed, the files will be formed of four men aligned, and elbow to elbow. The intervals will be preserved.

137. The file closers will also move by side step to the right, so that when the ranks are formed, they will be two paces from the rearmost rank.

138. At the command *march*, the company will move off briskly in quick time; the covering sergeant at the head of the front rank, and the captain on his left, will march straight forward. The men of each file will march abreast of their respective front rank men, heads direct to the front; the file closers will march opposite their places in line of battle.

139. The instructor will cause the principles of the march by the flank to be observed, in placing himself, pending the march, as prescribed in the school of the soldier, No. 357.

140. The instructor will cause the march by the left flank to be executed by the same commands, substituting *left* for *right*; the ranks will double as has been prescribed in the school for the soldier, No. 354; the rear rank will side-step to the left one pace before doubling.

141. At the instant the company faces to the left, the left guide will place   at   ain will

pass rapidly to the left, and place himself by the right side of this guide; the covering sergeant will replace the captain in the front rank, the moment the latter quits it to go to the left.

ARTICLE II.—*To change direction by file.*

142. The company being faced by the flank, and either in march or at a halt, when the instructor shall wish to cause it to wheel by file, he will command:

1. *By file, left,* (or *right*). 2. MARCH.

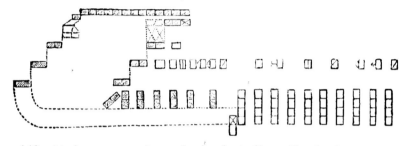

143. At the command *march*, the first file will wheel; if to the side of the front rank man, the latter will take care not to turn at once, but to describe a short arc of a circle, shortening a little the first five or six steps in order to give time to the fourth man of this file to conform himself to the movement. If the wheel be to the side of the rear rank, the front rank man will wheel in the step of twenty-eight inches, and the fourth man will conform himself to the movement by describing a short arc of a circle as has been explained. Each file will come to wheel on the same ground where that which preceded it wheeled.

144. The instructor will see that the wheel be executed according to these principles, in order that the distance between the files may always be preserved, and that there be no check or hindrance at the wheeling point.

ARTICLE III.—*To halt the company marching by the flank, and to face it to the front.*

145. To effect these objects, the instructor will command:

1. *Company.* 2. HALT. 3. FRONT.

146. The second and third commands will be executed as prescribed in the school of the soldier, Nos. 359 and 360. As soon as the files have undoubled, the rear rank will close to its proper distance. The captain and covering sergeant, as well as the left guide, if the march be by the left flank, will return to their habitual places in line at the instant the company faces to the front.

147. The instructor may then align the company by one of the means prescribed, No. 100.

SCHOOL OF THE COMPANY. 61

ARTICLE IV.— *The company being in march by the flank, to form it on the right (or left) by file into line of battle*

148. If the company be marching by the right flank, the instructor will command.

1. *On the right, by file into line.* 2. MARCH

149. At the command *march*, the rear rank men doubled will mark time, the captain and the covering sergeant will turn to the right, march straight forward, and be halted by the instructor when they shall have passed at least six paces beyond the rank of file closers, the captain will place himself correctly on the line of battle, and will direct the alignment as the men of the front rank successively arrive; the covering sergeant will place himself behind the captain at the distance of the rear rank, the two men on the right of the front rank doubled, will continue to march, and passing beyond the covering sergeant and the captain, will turn to the right, after turning, they will continue to march elbow to elbow, and direct themselves towards the line of battle, but when they shall arrive at two paces from this line, the even number will shorten the step so that the odd number may precede him on the line, the odd number placing himself by the side and on the left of the captain, the even number will afterwards oblique to the left, and place himself on the left of the odd number; the next two men of the front rank doubled, will pass in the same manner behind the two first, turn then to the right, and place themselves, according to the means just explained, to the left, and by the side of, the two men already established on the line, the remaining files of this rank will follow in succession, and be formed to the left in the same manner. The rear rank doubled will execute the movement in the manner already explained for the front rank, taking care not to commence the movement until four men of the front rank are established on the line of battle, the rear rank men, as they arrive on the line, will cover accurately their file leaders.

150. If the company be marching by the left flank, the instructor will cause it to form by file on the left into line of battle, according to the same principles and by the same commands, substituting the indication *left* for *right*. In this case, the odd numbers will shorten the step, so that the even numbers may precede them on the line. The captain, placed on the left of the front rank, and the left guide, will return to their places in line of battle, by order of the instructor, after the company shall be formed and aligned.

151. To enable the men the better to comprehend the mechanism of this movement, the instructor will at first cause it to be executed separately by each rank doubled, and afterwards by the two ranks united and doubled.

152. The instructor will place himself on the line of battle, and without the point where the right or left is to rest, in order to

establish the base of the alignment, and afterwards, he will follow up the movement to assure himself that each file conforms itself to what is prescribed No. 149.

ARTICLE V.—*The company being in march by the flank, to form it by company, or by platoon, into line, and to cause it to face to the right and left in marching.*

153. The company being in march by the right flank, the instructor will order the captain to form it into line; the captain will immediately command:

1. *By company, into line.* 2. MARCH.

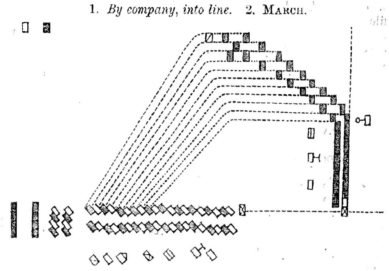

154. At the command *march*, the covering sergeant will continue to march straight forward; the men will advance the right shoulder, take the double quick step, and move into line, by the shortest route, taking care to undouble the files, and to come on the line one after the other.

155. As the front rank men successively arrive in line with the covering sergeant, they will take from him the step, and then turn their eyes to the front.

156. The men of the rear rank will conform to the movements of their respective file leaders, but without endeavoring to arrive in line at the same time with the latter.

157. At the instant the movement begins, the captain will face to his company in order to follow up the execution; and, as soon as the company is formed, he will command, *guide left*, place himself two paces before the center, face to the front, and take the step of the company.

158. At the command *guide left*, the second sergeant will promptly place himself in the front rank, on the left, to serve as guide, and the covering sergeant who is on the opposite flank will remain there.

159. When the company marches by the left flank, this movement will be executed by the same commands, and according to the same principles; the company being formed, the captain will command *guide right*, and place himself in front of his company as above; the covering sergeant who is on the right of the front rank will serve as guide, and the second sergeant placed on the left flank will remain there

160. Thus, in a column by company, right or left in front, the covering sergeant and the second sergeant of each company will always be placed on the right and left, respectively, of the front rank, they will be denominated *right guide* and *left guide*, and the one or the other charged with the direction

161. The company being in march by the flank, if it be the wish of the instructor to cause it to form platoons, he will give an order to that effect to the captain, who will command

1. *By platoon, into line.* 2. MARCH.

162. The movement will be executed by each platoon according to the above principles. The captain will place himself before the center of the first platoon, and the first lieutenant before the center of the second, passing through the opening made in the center of the company, if the march be by the right flank, and around the left of his platoon, if the march be by the left; in this last case the captain will also pass around the left of the second platoon in order to place himself in front of the first. Both the captain and lieutenant, without waiting for each other, will command *guide left* (or *right*) at the instant their respective platoons are formed.

163. At the command *guide left* (or *right*) the guide of each platoon will pass rapidly to the indicated flank of the platoon, if not already there

164. The right guide of the company will always serve as the guide of the right or left of the first platoon, and the left guide of the company will serve, in like manner, as the guide of the second platoon

165. Thus in a column, by platoon, there will be but one guide to each platoon; he will always be placed on its left flank, if the right be in front, and on the right flank, if the left be in front

166. In these movements the file closers will follow the platoons to which they are attached.

167. The instructor will cause the company, marching by the flank, to form by company, or by platoon, into line, by his own direct commands, using those prescribed for the captain, No. 153 or 161.

168. The instructor will exercise the company in passing, without a halt, from the march by the front, to the march by the flank, and reciprocally. In either case, he will employ the commands prescribed in the School of the Soldier, No. 363, substituting *company* for *squad*. The company will face to the right or left in marching, and the captain, the guides, and file closers will conform themselves to what is prescribed for each in the

flank, or in the march by the front of a company supposed to be a subdivision of a column.

169. If, after facing to the right or left, in marching, the company find itself faced by the rear rank, the captain will place himself two paces behind the center of the front rank, now in the rear, the guides will pass to the rear rank, now leading, and the file closers will march in front of this rank.

170. The instructor, in order to avoid fatiguing the men, and to prevent them from being negligent in the position of shoulder arms, will sometimes order support arms in marching by the flank, and arms on the right shoulder, when marching in line.

LESSON FIFTH.

Article I.—*To break into column by platoon, either at a halt or in march.*

171. The company being at a halt, in line of battle, the instructor, wishing to break it into column, by platoon to the right, will command:

1. *By platoon, right wheel.* 2. March.

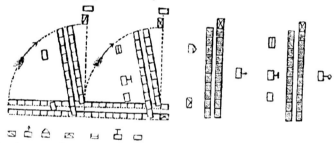

172. At the first command, the chiefs of platoon will rapidly place themselves two paces before the centers of their respective platoons, the lieutenant passing around the left of the company. They need not occupy themselves with dressing, one upon the other. The covering sergeant will replace the captain in the front rank.

173. At the command *march*, the right front rank man of each platoon will face to the right, the covering sergeant standing fast; the chief of each platoon will move quickly by the shortest line, a little beyond the point at which the marching flank will rest when the wheel shall be completed, face to the late rear, and place himself so that the line which he forms with the man on the right (who had faced,) shall be perpendicular to that occupied by the company in line of battle; each platoon will wheel according to the principles prescribed for the wheel on a fixed pivot, and when the man who conducts the marching flank shall approach near to the perpendicular, its chief will command:

1. *Platoon.* 2. Halt.

174. At the command *halt*, which will be given at the instant

SCHOOL OF THE COMPANY.

the man who conducts the marching flank shall have arrived at three paces from the perpendicular, the platoon will halt; the covering sergeant will move to the point where the left of the first platoon is to rest, passing by the front rank, the second sergeant will place himself, in like manner, in respect to the second platoon. Each will take care to leave between himself and the man on the right of his platoon, a space equal to its front, the captain and first lieutenant will look to this, and each take care to align the sergeant between himself and the man of the platoon who had faced to the right.

175. The guide of each platoon being thus established on the perpendicular, each chief will place himself two paces outside of his guide, and facing towards him, will command:

3 *Left*—DRESS

176. The alignment being ended, each chief of platoon will command, *Front*, and place himself two paces before its center.

177. The file closers will conform themselves to the movement of their respective platoons, preserving always the distance of two paces from the rear rank.

178. The company will break by platoon to the left, according to the same principles. The instructor will command:

1 *By platoon, left wheel* 2 MARCH

179. The first command will be executed in the same manner as if breaking by platoon to the right.

180. At the command *march*, the left front rank man of each platoon will face to the left, and the platoons will wheel to the left, according to the principles prescribed for the wheel on a fixed pivot, the chiefs of platoon will conform to the principles indicated Nos. 173 and 174.

181. At the command *halt*, given by the chief of each platoon, the covering sergeant on the right of the front rank of the first platoon, and the second sergeant near the left of the second platoon, will each move to the points where the right of his platoon is to rest. The chief of each platoon should be careful to align the sergeant between himself and the man of the platoon who had faced to the left, and will then command

Right—DRESS.

182. The platoons being aligned, each chief of platoon will command *Front*, and place himself opposite its center.

183. The instructor wishing to break the company by platoon to the right and to move the column forward after the wheel is completed, will caution the company to that effect, and command:

1. *By platoon, right wheel* 2 MARCH

184. At the first command the chiefs of platoon will move rapidly in front of their respective platoons, conforming to what has been prescribed No. 172, and will remain in this position during the

continuance of the wheel. The covering sergeant will replace the chief of the first platoon in the front rank.

185. At the command *march*, the platoons will wheel to the right, conforming to the principles herein prescribed, the man on the pivot will not face to the right, but will mark time, conforming himself to the movement of the marching flank, and when the man who is on the left of this flank shall arrive near the perpendicular, the instructor will command

3 *Forward* 4 MARCH. 5 *Guide left*

186. At the fourth command, which will be given at the instant the wheel is completed, the platoons will move straight to the front, all the men taking the step of twenty-eight inches. The covering sergeant and the second sergeant will move rapidly to the left of their respective platoons, the former passing before the front rank The leading guide will immediately take points on the ground in the direction which may be indicated to him by the instructor

187 At the fifth command, the men will take the touch of elbows lightly to the left

188. If the guide of the second platoon should lose his distance, or the line of direction, he will conform to the principles herein prescribed, Nos 202 and 203.

189 If the company be marching in line to the front, the instructor will cause it to break by platoon to the right by the same commands At the command *march*, the platoons will wheel in the manner already explained; the man on the pivot will take care to mark time in his place, without advancing or receding, the instructor, the chiefs of platoon, and the guides, will conform to what has been prescribed Nos. 184 and following.

190 The company may be broken by platoons to the left, according to the same principles, and by inverse means, the instructor giving the commands prescribed Nos. 183 and 185, substituting *left* for *right*, and reciprocally

191 The movements explained in Nos 183 and 189 will only be executed after the company has become well established in the principles of the march in column, Articles Second and Third

Remarks.

192 The instructor, placed in front of the company, will observe whether the movement be executed according to the principles prescribed above, whether the platoons, after breaking into column, are perpendicular to the line of battle just occupied, and whether the guide, who placed himself where the marching flank of his platoon had to rest, has left, between himself and the front rank man on the right (or left), the space necessary to contain the front of the platoon

193 After the platoons have broken, if the rearmost guard should not accurately cover the leading one, he will not seek to correct his position till the column be put in march, unless the instructor wishing to wheel immediately into line, should think it necessary

to rectify the direction of the guides, which would be executed as will be hereinafter explained in Article Fifth of this Lesson

194. The instructor will observe, that the man on the right (or left) of each platoon, who, at the command *march*, faces to the right (or left) being the true pivot of the wheel, the front rank man next to him ought to gain a little ground to the front in wheeling, so as clear the pivot-man.

ARTICLE II.—*To march in column.*

195. The company having broken by platoon, right (or left) in front, the instructor, wishing to cause the column to march, will throw himself twenty-five or thirty paces in front, face to the guides, place himself correctly, on their direction, and caution the leading guide to take points on the ground

196. The instructor being thus placed, the guide of the leading platoon will take two points on the ground in the straight line passing between his own and the heels of the instructor

197. These dispositions being made, the instructor will step aside and command

1 *Column, forward.*   2 *Guide left (or right).*   3 MARCH.

198. At the command *march*, promptly repeated by the chiefs of platoon, they, as well as the guides, will lead off, by a decided step, their respective platoons, in order that the whole may move smartly, and at the same moment.

199. The men will each feel lightly the elbow of his neighbor toward the guide, and conform himself, in marching, to the principles prescribed in the school of the soldier, No 327 The man next to the guide, in each platoon, will take care never to pass him, and also to march always about six inches to the right (or left) from him, in order not to push him out of the direction.

200. The leading guide will observe, with the greatest precision, the length and cadence of the step, and maintain the direction of his march by the means prescribed No. 89.

201. The following guide will march exactly in the trace of the leading one, preserving between the latter and himself a distance precisely equal to the front of his platoon, and marching in the same step with the leading guide

202. If the following guide lose his distance from the one leading, (which can only happen by his own fault,) he will correct himself by slightly lengthening or shortening a few steps, in order that there may not be sudden quickenings or slackenings in the march of his platoon

203. If the same guide, having neglected to march exactly in the trace of the preceding one, find himself sensibly out of the direction, he will remedy this fault by advancing more or less the shoulder opposite to the true direction, and thus, in a few steps, insensibly regain it, without the inconvenience of the oblique step, which would cause a loss of distance In all cases, each chief of platoon w   uide.

Remarks on the march in column.

204. If the chiefs and guides of subdivisions neglect to lead off and to decide the march from the first step, the march will be begun in uncertainty, which will cause waverings, a loss of step and a loss of distance.

205. If the leading guide take unequal steps, the march of his subdivision, and that which follows will be uncertain, there will be undulations, quickenings, and slackenings in the march.

206. If the same guide be not habituated to prolong a given direction, without deviation, he will describe a crooked line, and the column must wind to conform itself to such line.

207. If the following guide be not habituated to march in the trace of the preceding one, he will lose his distance at every moment in endeavors to regain the trace, the preservation of which is the most important principle in the march in column

*208. The guide of each subdivision in column will be responsible for the direction, distance and step, the chief of the subdivision, for the order and conformity of his subdivision with the movements of the guide Accordingly, the chief will frequently turn, in the march, to observe his subdivision

209 The instructor, placed on the flank of the guides, will watch over the execution of all the principles prescribed, he will, also, sometimes place himself in the rear, align himself on the guides, and halt, pending some thirty paces together, to verify the accuracy of the guides.

210 In column, chiefs of subdivision will always repeat, with the greatest promptitude, the commands *march* and *halt*, no chief waiting for another, but each repeating the command the moment he catches it from the instructor. They will repeat no other command given by him, but will explain, if necessary, to their subdivisions, in an under tone of voice, what they will have to execute, as indicated by the commands of caution.

Article III.—*To change direction.*

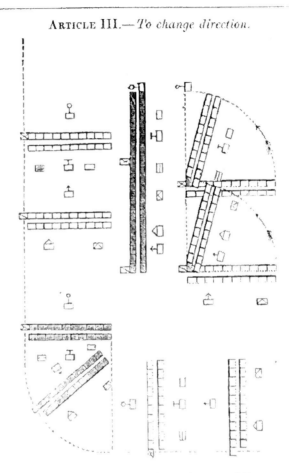

211. The changes of direction of a column while marching, will be executed according to the principles prescribed for wheeling on the march. Whenever, therefore, a column is to change direction, the instructor will change the guide, if not already there, to the flank opposite the side to which the change is to be made.

212. The column being in march right in front, if it be the wish of the instructor to change direction to the right, he will give the order to the chief of the first platoon, and immediately go himself, or send a marker to the point at which the change of direction is to be made; the instructor, or marker, will place himself on the direction of the guides, so as to present the breast to that flank of the column.

213. The leading guide will direct his march on that person, so that, in passing, his left arm may just graze his breast. When the leading guide shall have approached near to the marker, the chief of his platoon will command:

SCHOOL OF THE COMPANY.

1 *Right wheel*   2 March

214 The first command will be given when the platoon is at the distance of four paces from the marker.

215 At the command *march*, which will be pronounced at the instant the guide shall have arrived opposite the marker, the platoon will wheel to the right, conforming to what is prescribed in the school of the soldier, No 396

216 The wheel being finished, the chief of each platoon will command

3 *Forward*   4 March

217. These commands will be pronounced and executed as is prescribed in the school of the soldier, Nos. 398 and 399. The guide of the first platoon will take points on the ground in the new direction, in order the better to regulate the march

218. The second platoon will continue to march straight forward till up with the marker, when it will wheel to the right, and retake the direct march by the same commands and the same means which governed the first platoon

219 The column being in march right in front, if the instructor should wish to change direction to the left, he will command, *guide right*   At this command, the two guides will move rapidly to the right of their respective platoons, each passing in front of his subdivision; the men will take the touch of elbows to the right; the instructor will afterwards conform to what is prescribed No 212.

220. The change of direction to the left will then be executed according to the same principles as the change of direction to the right, but by inverse means

221. When the change of direction is completed, the instructor will command, *guide left*

222 The changes of direction in a column, left in front, will be executed according to the same principles

223. In changes of direction in double quick time, the platoons will wheel according to the principles prescribed in the school of the soldier, No 401

224. In order to prepare the men for those formations in line, which can be executed only by turning to the right or the left, the instructor will sometimes cause the column to change direction to the side of the guide. In this case, the chief of the leading platoon will command   *Left* (or *right*) *turn*, instead of *left* (or *right*) *wheel*. The subdivisions will each turn, in succession, conforming to what is prescribed in the school of the soldier, No. 402 The leading guide, as soon as he has turned, will take points on the ground, the better to regulate the direction of the march.

225. It is highly important, in order to preserve distances and the direction, that all the subdivisions of the column should change direction precisely at the point where the leading subdivision changed, it is for this reason that that point ought to be marked

in advance, and that it is prescribed that the guides direct their march on the marker, also that each chief of subdivision shall not cause the change to commence till the guide of his subdivision has grazed the breast of this marker.

226. Each chief will take care that his subdivision arrives at the point of change in a square with the line of direction, with this view, he will face to his subdivision when the one which precedes has commenced to turn or to wheel, and he will be watchful that it continues to march squarely until it arrives at the point where the change of direction is to commence.

227. If, in changes of direction, the pivot of the subdivision which wheels should not clear the wheeling point, the next subdivision would be arrested and distances lost, for the guide who conducts the marching flank having to describe an arc, in length about a half greater than the front of the subdivision, the second subdivision would be already up with the wheeling point, whilst the first which wheels has yet the half of its front to execute, and hence would be obliged to mark time until that half be executed. It is therefore prescribed, that the pivot of each subdivision should take steps of nine or eleven inches in length, according to the swiftness of the gait, in order not to arrest the march of the next subdivision. The chiefs of subdivision will look well to the step of the pivot, and cause his step to be lengthened or shortened as may be judged necessary. By the nature of this movement, the center of each subdivision will bend a little to the rear.

228. The guides will never alter the length or the cadence of the step, whether the change of direction be to the side of the guide or to the opposite side.

229. The marker, placed at the wheeling point, will always present his breast to the flank of the column. The instructor will take the greatest pains in causing the prescribed principles to be observed, he will see that each subdivision only commences the change of direction when the guide, grazing the breast of the marker, has nearly passed him, and, that the marching flank does not describe the arc of too large a circle, in order that it may not be thrown beyond the new direction.

230. In change of direction by wheel, the guide of the wheeling flank will cast his eyes over the ground at the moment of commencing the wheel, and will describe an arc of a circle whose radius is equal to the front of the subdivision.

ARTICLE IV.—*To halt the column.*

231. The column being in march, when the instructor shall wish to halt it he will command

1. *Column.* 2. HALT

232. At the second command, promptly repeated by the chiefs of platoon, the column will halt, the guides will also stand fast, although they may have lost the distance and direction

233. If the command *halt*, be not repeated with the greatest vivacity, and executed at the same instant, distances will be lost.

234. If a guide, having lost his distance, seek to recover it after that command, he will only throw his fault on the following guide, who, if he have marched well, will no longer be at his proper distance, and if the latter regain what he has thus lost, the movement will be propagated to the rear of the column.

ARTICLE V.—*Being in column by platoon, to form to the right or left into line of battle, either at a halt or on the march*

235. The instructor having halted the column, right in front, and wishing to form it into line of battle, will place himself at platoon distance in front of the leading guide, face to him, and rectify, if necessary, the position of the guide beyond; which being executed, he will command

Left—DRESS

236. At this command, which will not be repeated by the chiefs of platoon, each of them will place himself briskly two paces outside of his guide, and direct the alignment of the platoon perpendicularly to the direction of the column

237. Each chief having aligned his platoon, will command FRONT, and return quickly to his place in column

238. This disposition being made, the instructor will command.

1 *Left into line, wheel.* 2 MARCH

239. At the command march, briskly repeated by the chiefs of platoon, the front rank man on the left of each platoon will face to the left, and place his breast lightly against the arm of the guide by his side, who stands fast; the platoons will wheel to the left on the principle of wheels from a halt, and in conformity to what is prescribed No. 194. Each chief will turn to his platoon, to observe its movement, and when the marching flank has approached near the line of battle, he will command

1 *Platoon.* 2. HALT.

240. The command *halt*, will be given when the marching flank of the platoon is three paces from the line of battle.

241. The chief of the second platoon, having halted it, will return to his place as a file closer, passing around the left of his subdivision

242. The captain having halted the first platoon, will move rapidly to the point at which the right of the company will rest in line of battle and command

Right—DRESS

243. At this command, the two platoons will dress up on the alignment; the front rank man on the right of the leading platoon, who finds himself opposite the instructor established on the direction of the guides, will place his breast lightly against the

SCHOOL OF THE COMPANY.

left arm of this officer. The captain will direct the alignment from the right on the man on the opposite flank of the company.

244. The company being aligned, the captain will command:

FRONT

245. The instructor, seeing the company in line of battle, will command

Guides—POSTS.

246. At this command, the covering sergeant will cover the captain, and the left guide will return to his place as a file closer.

247. If the column be left in front, and the instructor should wish to form it to the right into line of battle, he will place himself at platoon distance in front of the leading guide, face to him, and rectify, if necessary, the position of the guide beyond; which being executed, he will command

1. *Right into line, wheel* 2. MARCH.

248. At the command *march*, the front rank man on the right of each platoon will face to the right and place his breast lightly against the left arm of the guide by his side, who stands fast, each platoon will wheel to the right, and will be halted by its chief, when the marching flank has approached near the line of battle; for this purpose, the chief of each platoon will command

1. *Platoon* 2. HALT.

249. The command *halt*, will be given when the marching flank of the platoon is three paces from the line of battle. The chief of the second platoon having halted his platoon, will resume his place in the rank of file closers.

250. The captain having halted the first platoon, will move briskly to the point at which the left of the company will rest, and command:

Left—DRESS.

251. At this command, the two platoons will dress up on the alignment; the man on the left of the second platoon, opposite the instructor, will place his breast lightly against the right arm of this officer, and the captain will direct the alignment from the left on the man on the opposite flank of the company.

252. The company being aligned, the captain will command

FRONT

253. The instructor will afterwards command

Guides—POSTS.

254. At this command, the captain will move to the right of his company, the covering sergeant will cover him and the left guide will return to his place as a file closer.

255. The instructor may omit the command *left* or *right dress*, previous t   ss, after

rectifying the position of the guides, it should become necessary to dress the platoons, or one of them, laterally to the right or left.

256. The instructor, before the command *left* (or *right*) *into line, wheel,* will assure himself that the rearmost platoon is at its exact wheeling distance from the one in front. This attention is important, in order to detect negligence on the part of guides in this essential point

257 If the column be marching right in front, and the instructor should wish to form it into line without halting the column, he will give the commands prescribed No 238, and move rapidly to platoon distance in front of the leading guide

258. At the command *march*, briskly repeated by the chiefs of platoon, the left guides will halt short, the instructor, the chiefs of platoon, and the platoons, will conform to what is prescribed No 239 and following.

259. If the column be in march left in front, this formation will be made according to the same principles, and by inverse means:

260. If the column be marching right in front, and the instructor should wish to form it into line without halting the column, and to march the company in line to the front, he will command

1. *By platoons left wheel.* 2. MARCH

261. At the command *march*, briskly repeated by the chiefs of platoon, the left guides will halt, the man next to the left guide in each platoon will mark time, the platoons will wheel to the left, conforming to the principles of a wheel on a fixed pivot. When the right of the platoons shall arrive near the line of battle, the instructor will command

3 *Forward.* 4 MARCH 5 *Guide right* (or *left*)

262. At the fourth command, given at the instant the wheel is completed, all the men of the company will move off together with the step of twenty-eight inches ; the captain, the chief of the second platoon, the covering sergeant, and the left guide will take their positions as in line of battle

263 At the fifth command, which will be given immediately after the fourth, the captain and covering sergeant, if not already there, will move briskly to the side on which the guide is designated The non-commissioned officer charged with the direction will move rapidly in front of the guide, and will be assured in his line of march by the instructor, as is prescribed No. 104. That non-commissioned officer will immediately take points on the ground as indicated in the same number The men will take the touch of elbows to the side of the guide, conforming themselves to the principles of the march in line.

264. The same principles are applicable to a column left in front

SCHOOL OF THE COMPANY.   75

LESSON SIXTH.

ARTICLE I.—*To break the company into platoons, and to reform the company.*

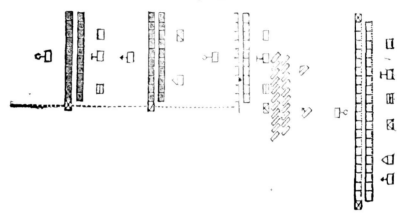

To break the company into platoons.

265. The company marching in the cadenced step, and supposed to make part of a column, right in front, when the instructor shall wish to cause it to break by platoon, he will give the order to the captain, who will command: 1. *Break into platoons*, and immediately place himself before the center of the first platoon.

266. At the command *break into platoons*, the first lieutenant will pass quickly around the left to the center of his platoon, and give the caution: *Mark time*.

267. The captain will then command: 2. *March*.

268. The first platoon will continue to march straight forward; the covering sergeant will move rapidly to the left flank of this platoon (passing by the front rank) as soon as the flank shall be disengaged.

269. At the command *march*, given by the captain, the second platoon will begin to mark time; its chief will immediately add: 1. *Right oblique*. 2. MARCH. The last command will be given so that this platoon may commence obliquing the instant the rear rank of the first platoon shall have passed. The men will shorten the step in obliquing, so that when the command *forward march* is given, the platoon may have its exact distance.

270. The guide of the second platoon being near the direction of the guide of the first, the chief of the second will command *Forward*, and add MARCH, the instant that the guide of his platoon shall cover the guide of the first.

271. In a column, left in front, the company will break into platoons by inverse means, applying to the first platoon all that has been prescribed for the second, and reciprocally.

272. In th... case the l... ...company ... ... to the

right flank of the second platoon, and the covering sergeant will remain on the right of the first

To re-form the company

273. The column, by platoon, being in march, right in front, when the instructor shall wish to cause it to form company, he will give order to the captain, who will command *Form company*

274. Having given this command, the captain will immediately add: 1. *First platoon* 2. *Right oblique.*

275. The chief of the second platoon will caution it to continue to march straight forward

276. The captain will then command 3. MARCH

277 At this command, repeated by the chief of the second, the first platoon will oblique to the right, in order to unmask the second, the covering sergeant, on the left of the first platoon, will return to the right of the company, passing by the front rank

278 When the first platoon shall have nearly unmasked the second, the captain will command 1 *Mark time*, and at the instant the unmasking shall be complete, he will add 2. MARCH The first platoon will then cease to oblique, and mark time

279 In the mean time the second platoon will have continued to march straight forward, and when it shall be nearly up with the first, the captain will command *Forward*, and at the instant the two platoons shall unite, add MARCH; the first platoon will then cease to mark time.

280. In a column, left in front, the same movement will be executed by inverse means. the chief of the second platoon giving the command *Forward*, and the captain adding the command MARCH, when the platoons are united.

281. The guide of the second platoon, on its right, will pass to its left flank the moment the platoons begin to oblique, the guide of the first, on its right, remaining on that flank of the platoon

282 The instructor will also sometimes cause the company to break and reform, by platoon, by his own direct commands. In this case, he will give the general commands prescribed for the captain above 1 *Break into platoons*, 2. MARCH and 1 *Form company*, 2. MARCH

283 If, in breaking the company into platoons, the subdivision that breaks off should mark time too long, it might, in a column of many subdivisions, arrest the march of the following one, which would cause a lengthening of the column, and a loss of distances

284 In breaking into platoons, it is necessary that the platoons which oblique should not shorten the step too much, in order not to lose distance in column, and not to arrest the march of the following subdivision.

285. If a platoon obliques too far to a flank, it would be obliged to oblique again to the opposite flank, to regain the direction, and by the double movement arrest. probably, the march of the following subdivision.

286. The chiefs of those platoons which oblique will face to their platoons, in order to enforce the observance of the foregoing principles.

287. When, in a column of several companies, they break in succession, it is of the greatest importance that each company should continue to march in the same step, without shortening or slackening, whilst that which precedes breaks, although the following company should close up on the preceding one. This attention is essential to guard against an elongation of the column.

288. Faults of but little moment, in a column of a few companies, would be serious inconveniences in a general column of many battalions. Hence the instructor will give the greatest care in causing all the prescribed principles to be strictly observed. To this end, he will hold himself on the directing flank, the better to observe all the movements.

ARTICLE II.—*Being in column, to break files to the rear, and to cause them to re-enter into line.*

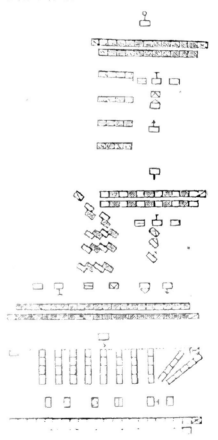

289. The company being in march, and supposed to constitute a subdivision of a column, right (or left) in front, when the instructor shall wish to cause files to break off he will give the order to the captain, who will immediately turn to his company, and command:

1. *Two files from left (or right) to rear.* 2. MARCH.

290. At the command *march*, the two files on the left (or right) of the company, will mark time, the others will continue to march straight forward; the two rear rank men of these files will, as soon as the rear rank of the company shall clear them, move to the right by advancing the outer shoulder; the odd number will place himself behind the third file from that flank, the even number behind the fourth, passing for this purpose behind the odd number; the two front rank men will, in like manner, move to the right when the rear rank of the company shall them, the odd number

place himself behind the first file, the even number behind the second file, passing for this purpose behind the odd number. If the files are broken from the right, the men will move to the left, advancing the outer shoulder, the even number of the rear rank will place himself behind the third file, the odd number of the same rank behind the fourth, the even number of the front rank behind the first file, the odd number of the same rank behind the second, the odd numbers for this purpose passing behind the even numbers. The men will be careful not to lose their distances and to keep aligned.

291. If the instructor should still wish to break two files from the same side, he will give the order to the captain, who will proceed as above directed.

292. At the command *march*, given by the captain, the files already broken, advancing a little the outer shoulder, will gain the space of two files to the right, if the files are broken from the left, and to the left, if the files are broken from the right, shortening, at the same time, the step, in order to make room between themselves and the rear rank of the company for the files last ordered to the rear; the latter will break by the same commands and in the same manner as the first. The men who double should increase the length of the step in order to prevent distances from being lost.

293. The instructor may thus diminish the front of a company by breaking off successive groups of two files, but the new files must always be broken from the same side.

294. The instructor, wishing to cause files broken off to return into line, will give the order to the captain, who will immediately command:

1. *Two files into line.* 2. MARCH.

295. At the command *march*, the first two files of those marching by the flank will return briskly into line, and the others will gain the space of two files by advancing the inner shoulder towards the flank to which they belong.

296. The captain will turn to his company, to watch the observance of the principles which have just been prescribed.

297. The instructor having caused groups of two files to break one after another, and to return again into line, will afterwards cause two or three groups to break together, and for this purpose, will command: *Four or six files from left (or right) to rear;* MARCH. The files designated will mark time, each rank will advance a little the outer shoulder as soon as the rear rank of the company shall clear it, will oblique at once, and each group will place itself behind the four neighboring files, and in the same manner, as if the movement had been executed group by group, taking care that the distances are preserved.

298. The instructor will next order the captain to cause two or three groups to be brought into line at once, who turning to the company, will command:

SCHOOL OF THE COMPANY.

Four or six file into line—MARCH

299. At the command *march*, the files designated will advance the inner shoulder, move up and form on the flank of the company by the shortest lines.

300. As often as files shall break off to the rear, the guide on that flank will gradually close on the nearest front rank man remaining in line, and he will also open out to make room for files ordered into line.

301. The files which march in the rear are disposed in the following order: the left files as if the company was marching by the right flank, and the right files as if the company was marching by the left flank. Consequently, whenever there is on the right or left of a subdivision, a file which does not belong to a group, it will be broken singly.

302. It is necessary to the preservation of distances in column that the men should be habituated in the schools of detail to execute the movements of this article with precision.

303. If new files broken off do not step well to the left or right in obliquing; if, when files are ordered into line, they do not move up with promptitude and precision, in either case the following files will be arrested in their march, and thereby cause the column to be lengthened out.

304. The instructor will place himself on the flank from which the files are broken, to assure himself of the exact observance of the principles.

305. Files will only be broken off from the side of direction, in order that the whole company may easily pass from the front to the flank march.

ARTICLE III—*To march the column in route, and to execute the movements incident thereto.*

306. The swiftness of the route step will be one hundred and ten steps in a minute; this swiftness will be habitually maintained in columns in route, when the roads and ground may permit.

307. The company being at a halt, and supposed to constitute a subdivision of a column, when the instructor shall wish to cause it to march in the route step he will command:

1. *Column, forward.* 2. *Guide left* (or *right*) 3. *Route step*
4. MARCH.

308. At the command *march*, repeated by the captain, the two ranks will step off together; the rear rank will take, in marching, by shortening a few steps, a distance of one pace (twenty-eight inches) from the rank preceding, which distance will be computed from the breasts of the men in the rear rank, to the knapsacks of the men in the front rank. The men, without further command, will immediately carry their arms *at will*, as indicated in the School of the Soldier, No. 219. They will no longer be required to match in the

silent The files will march at ease, but care will be taken to prevent the ranks from intermixing, the front rank from getting in advance of the guide, and the rear rank from opening to too great a distance.

309. The company marching in the route step, the instructor will cause it to change direction, which will be executed without formal commands, on a simple caution from the captain, the rear rank will come up to change direction in the same manner as the front rank Each rank will conform itself, although in the route step, to the principles which have been prescribed for the change in closed ranks, with this difference only, that the pivot man, instead of taking steps of nine, will take steps of fourteen inches, in order to clear the wheeling point.

310 The company marching in the route step, to cause it to pass to the cadenced step, the instructor will first order pieces to be brought to the right shoulder, and then command.

1 *Quick time.* 2. MARCH.

311 At the command *march*, the men will resume the cadenced step, and will close so as to leave a distance of sixteen inches between each rank

312 The company marching in the cadenced pace, the instructor, to cause it to take the route step will command

1. *Route step.* 2. MARCH.

313 At the command *march*, the front rank will continue the step of twenty-eight inches, the rear rank will take, by gradually shortening the step, the distance of twenty-eight inches from the front rank, the men will carry their arms at will.

314 If the company be marching in the route step, and the instructor should suppose the necessity of marching by the flank in the same direction, he will command

1 *Company by the right* (or *left*) *flank* 2. *By file left* (or *right*) 3. MARCH.

315. At the command *march*, the company will face to the right (or left) in marching, the captain will place himself by the side of the guide who conducts the leading flank; this guide will wheel immediately to the left or right, all the files will come in succession to wheel on the same spot as the guide, if there be files broken off to the rear, they will, by wheeling, regain their respective places, and follow the movement of the company.

316 The instructor having caused the company to be again formed into line, will exercise it in increasing and diminishing front, by platoon, which will be executed by the same commands and the same means, as if the company were marching in the cadenced step. When the company breaks into platoons, the chief of each will move to the flank of his platoon, and will take the place of the guide, who will step back into the rear rank.

317 The company being in column by platoon, and supposed to

march in the route step, the instructor can cause the front to be diminished and increased, by section, if the platoons have a front of twelve files or more

318. The movements of diminishing and increasing front, by section, will be executed according to the principles indicated for the same movements by platoon. The right sections of platoons will be commanded by the captain and first lieutenant, respectively; the left sections by the two next subalterns in rank, or, in their absence, by sergeants.

319. The instructor wishing to diminish by section, will give the order to the captain, who will command

1. *Break into sections.* 2. MARCH.

320. As soon as the platoons shall be broken, each chief of section will place himself on its directing flank in the front rank; the guides who will be thus displaced, will fall back into the rear rank; the file closers will close up to within one pace of this rank.

321. Platoons will be broken into sections only in the column in route; the movement will never be executed in the manœuvres, whatever may be the front of the company.

322. When the instructor shall wish to reform platoons, he will give the order to the captain, who will command

1 *Form platoons.* 2 MARCH.

323. At the first command, each chief of sections will place himself before its center, and the guides will pass into the front rank. At the command *march*, the movement will be executed as has been prescribed for forming company. The moment the platoons are formed, the chiefs of the left sections will return to their places as file closers.

324. The instructor will also cause to be executed the diminishing and increasing front by files, as prescribed in the preceding article, and in the same manner, as if marching in the cadenced step. When the company is broken into sections, the subdivisions must not be reduced to a front of less than six files, not counting the chief of the section.

325. The company being broken by platoon or by section, the instructor will cause it, marching in the route step, to march by the flank in the same direction, by the commands and the means indicated, Nos 314 and 315. The moment the subdivisions shall face to the right (or left,) the first file of each will wheel to the left (or right,) in marching, to prolong the direction, and to unite with the rear file of the subdivision immediately preceding. The file closers will take their habitual places in the march by the flank, before the union of the subdivisions.

326. If the company be marching by the right flank, and the instructor should wish to undouble the files, which might sometimes be found necessary, he will inform the captain, who, after causing the cadenced step to be resumed, and arms to be shouldered or supported, will command

1. *In two ranks, undouble files.* 2. MARCH.

327. At the second command, the odd numbers will continue to march straight forward, the even numbers will shorten the step, and obliquing to the left will place themselves promptly behind the odd numbers; the rear rank will gain a step to the left, so as to retake the touch of elbows on the side of the front rank.

228. If the company be marching by the left flank, it will be the even numbers who will continue to march forward, and the odd numbers who will undouble.

329. If the instructor should wish to double the files, he will give the order to the captain, who will command

1. *In four ranks, double files.* 2 MARCH

330 At the command *march*, the files will double in the manner as explained, when the company faces by the right or the left flank The instructor will afterwards cause the route step to be resumed.

331 The various movements prescribed in this lesson may be executed in double quick time The men will be brought, by degrees, to pass over at this gait about eleven hundred yards in seven minutes.

332 When the company marching in the route step shall halt, the rear rank will close up at the command *halt*, and the whole will shoulder arms

333 Marching in the route step, the men will be permitted to carry their pieces in the manner they shall find most convenient, paying attention only to holding the muzzles up, so as to avoid accidents.

ARTICLE IV.—*Countermarch*

334 The company being at a halt, and supposed to constitute part of a column, right in front, when the instructor shall wish to cause it to countermarch, he will command·

1. *Countermarch.* 2. *Company, right*—FACE 3 *By file.left.* 4. MARCH

335. At the second command the company will face to the right, the two guides to the right about; the captain will go to the right of his company and cause two files to break to the rear, and then place himself by the side of the front rank man, to conduct him.

336 At the command *march*, both guides will stand fast, the company will step off smartly, the first file conducted by the captain, will wheel around the right guide, and direct its march along the front rank so as to arrive behind, and two paces from the left guide; each file will come in succession to wheel on the same ground around the right guide; the leading file having arrived at a point opposite to the left guide, the captain will command

1. *Company.* 2. HALT. 3. FRONT. 4. *Right*—DRESS.

337 The first command will be given at *four* paces from the po nt where the leading file is to rest.

338. At the second command, the company will halt.

339. At the third, it will face to the front.

340. At the fourth, the company will dress by the right; the captain will step two paces outside of the left guide, now on the right, and direct the alignment, so that the front rank may be enclosed between the two guides; the company being aligned, he will command FRONT, and place himself before the center of the company as if in column; the guides, passing along the front rank, will shift to their proper places, on the right and left of that rank.

341. In a column, by platoon, the countermarch will be executed by the same commands, and according to the same principles; the guide of each platoon will face about, and its chief will place himself by the side of the file on the right, to conduct it.

342. In a column, left in front, the countermarch will be executed by inverse commands and means, but according to the same principles. Thus, the movement will be made by the right flank of subdivisions, if the right be in front, and by the left flank, if the left be in front; in both cases the subdivisions will wheel by file to the side of the front rank.

ARTICLE V.—*Being in column by platoon, to form on the right (or left) into line of battle.*

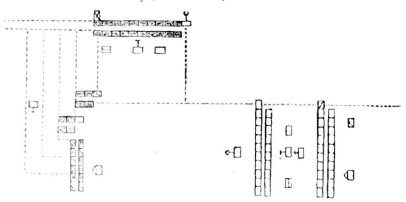

343. The column by platoon, right in front, being in march, the instructor, wishing to form it on the right into line of battle, will command:

1. *On the right into line.* 2. *Guide right.*

344. At the second command, the guide of each platoon will shift quickly to its right flank, and the men will touch elbows to the right; the column will continue to march straight forward.

345. The instructor having given the second command, will move briskly to the point at which the right of the company ought to rest in line, and place himself facing the point of direction to the left which he will choose.

346. The line of battle ought to be so chosen that the guide of each platoon, after having turned to the right, may have, at least, ten paces to take before arriving upon that line.

347. The head of the column being nearly opposite to the instructor, the chief of the first platoon will command 1 *Right turn*, and when exactly opposite to that point, he will add.

2 MARCH.

348. At the command *march* the first platoon will turn to the right, in conformity with the principles prescribed in the school of the soldier, No 402. Its guide will so direct his march as to bring the front rank man next on his left, opposite to the instructor; the chief of the platoon will march before its center, and when its guide shall be near the line of battle, he will command

1. *Platoon.* 2 HALT.

349. At the command *halt*, which will be given at the instant the right of the platoon shall arrive at the distance of three paces from the line of battle, the platoon will halt; the files, not yet in line, will come up promptly. The guide will throw himself on the line of battle, opposite to one of the three left files of his platoon, he will face to the instructor, who will align him on the point of direction to the left. The chief of platoon having, at the same time, gone to the point where the right of the company is to rest, will, as soon as he sees all the files of the platoon in line, command

Right—DRESS.

350. At this the first platoon will align itself; the front rank man, who finds himself opposite to the guide will rest his breast lightly against the right arm of this guide, and the chief of the platoon, from the right, will direct the alignment on this man

351. The second platoon will continue to march straight forward, until its guide shall arrive opposite to the left file of the first, it will then turn to the right at the command of its chief, and march towards the line of battle, its guide directing himself on the left file of the first platoon

352. The guide having arrived at the distance of three paces from the line of battle, this platoon will be halted, as prescribed for the first, at the instant it halts, its guide will spring on the line of battle, opposite to one of the three left files of his platoon, and will be assured in his position by the instructor

353. The chief of the second platoon, seeing all its files in line, and its guide established on the direction, will command

Right—DRESS

354. Having given this command, he will return to his place as a file closer, passing around the left, the second platoon will dress up on the alignment of the first, and, when established, the captain will command

FRONT

355. The movement ended, the instructor will command:

SCHOOL OF THE COMPANY.

Guides—Posts

356. At this command, the two guides will return to their places in line of battle.

357. A column, by platoon, left in front, will form on the left into line of battle, according to the same principles, and, by inverse means, applying to the second platoon what is prescribed for the first, and reciprocally. The chief of the second platoon having aligned it, from the point of *appui*, (the left,) will retire to his place as a file closer. The captain having halted the first platoon three paces behind the line of battle, will go to the same point to align this platoon, and then command · Front. At the command, *guides—posts*, given by the instructor, the captain will shift to his proper flank, and the guides take their places in the line of battle.

358. When the companies of a regiment are to be exercised, at the same time, in the school of the company, the colonel will indicate the lesson or lessons they are severally to execute. The whole will commence by a bugle signal, and terminate in like manner.

Formation of a company from two ranks into single rank, and reciprocally

359. The company being formed into two ranks, in the manner indicated No 8, school of the soldier, and supposed to make part of a column, right or left in front, when the instructor shall wish to form it into single rank, he will command

    1. *In one rank, form company.* 2. March.

360. At the first command, the right guide will face to the right.

361. At the command *march*, the right guide will step off and march in the prolongation of the front rank

362. The first file will step off at the same time with the guide; the front rank man will turn to the right at the first step, follow the guide, and be himself followed by the rear rank man of his file, who will come to turn on the same spot where he had turned. The second file, and successively all the other files, will step off as has been prescribed for the first, the front rank man of each file following immediately the rear rank man of the file next on his right. The captain will superintend the movement, and when the last man shall have stepped off, he will halt the company, and face it to the front

363. The file closers will take their places in the line of battle, two paces in the rear of the rank.

364. The company being in single rank, when the instructor shall wish to form it into two ranks, he will command:

    1. *In two ranks, form company.* 2. *Company, right*—Face.
    3 March.

365. At the second command, the company will face to the right; the right guide and the man on the right will remain faced to the front.

366. At the command *march*, the men who have faced to the right, will step off, and form files in the following manner. the second man in the rank will place himself behind the first to form the first file, the third will place himself by the side of the first in the front rank, the fourth behind the third in the rear rank. All the others will, in like manner, place themselves, alternately, in the front and rear rank, and will thus form files of two men, on the left of those already formed

367. The formations above described will be habitually executed by the right of companies, but when the instructor shall wish to have them executed by the left, he will face the company *about*, and post the guides in the rear rank.

368. The formation will then be executed by the same commands and according to the same principles as by the front rank; the movement commencing with the left file, now become the right, and in each file by the rear rank man. now become the front, the left guide will conform to what has been prescribed for the right

369. The formation ended, the instructor will face the company to its proper front.

370. When a battalion in line has to execute either of the formations above described, the colonel will cause it to break to the rear by the right or left of companies, and will then give the commands just prescribed for the instructor. Each company will execute the movement as if acting singly.

Formation of a company from two ranks into four, and reciprocally, at a halt, and in march

371 The company being formed in two ranks, at a halt, and supposed to form part of a column right in front, when the instructor shall wish to form it into four ranks, he will command

1. *In four ranks, form company* 2 *Company left*—FACE 3. MARCH
(or *double quick*—MARCH)

372. At the second command, the left guide will remain faced to the front, the company will face to the left, the rear rank will gain the distance of one pace from the front rank by a side step to the left and rear, and the men will form into four ranks as prescribed in the school of the soldier.

373 At the command *march*, the first file of four men will reface to the front without undoubling All the other files of four will step off, and closing successively to about five inches of the preceding file, will halt, and immediately face to the front, the men remaining doubled

374 The file closers will take their new places in line of battle, at two paces in rear of the fourth rank.

375 The captain will superintend the movement.

376. The company being in four ranks, when the instructor shall wish to form it into two ranks, he will command:

1. *In two ranks, form company.* 2. *Company right*—FACE. 3. MARCH
(or *double quick*—MARCH).

377. At the second command the left guide will stand fast, the company will face to the right.

378 At the command *march*, the right guide will step off and march in the prolongation of the front rank. The leading file of four men will step off at the same time, the other files standing fast; the second file will step off when there shall be between it and the first space sufficient to form into two ranks The following files will execute successively what has been prescribed for the second As soon as the last file shall have its distance, the instructor will command

1. *Company.* 2 HALT. 3 FRONT.

379 At the command *front*, the company will face to the front and the files will undouble.

380. The company being formed in two ranks, and marching to the front, when the instructor shall wish to form it into four ranks he will command.

1 *In four ranks, form company* 2. *By the left double files.* 3. MARCH
(or *double quick*—MARCH).

381 At the command *march*, the left guide and the left file of the company will continue to march straight to the front, the company will make a half face to the left, the odd numbers placing themselves behind the even numbers The even numbers of the rear rank will shorten their steps a little, to permit the odd numbers of the front rank to get between them and the even numbers of that rank The files thus formed of fours, except the left file, will continue to march obliquely, lengthening their steps slightly, so as to keep constantly abreast of the guide; each file will close successively on the file next on its left, and when at the proper distance from that file, will face to the front by a half face to the right, and take the touch of elbows to the left

382 The company being in march to the front in four ranks, when the instructor shall wish to form it into two ranks, he will command.

1 *In two ranks, form company.* 2. *By the right, undouble files* 3.
MARCH (or *double quick* MARCH)

383 At the command *march*, the left guide and the left file of the company will continue to march straight to the front; the company will make a half face to the right and march obliquely, lengthening the step a little, in order to keep, as near as possible, abreast of the guide As soon as the second file from the left shall have gained to the right the interval necessary for the left file to form into two ranks, the second file will face to the front by a half face to the left and march straight forward the left file will immediately t a   tw r   f l   t   ows to

the left. Each file will execute successively, what has just been prescribed for the file next to the left, and each file will form into two ranks when the file next on its right has obliqued the required distance and faced to the front.

384. If the company be supposed to make part of a column, left in front, these different movements will be executed according to the same principles and by inverse means, substituting the indication *left* for *right*.

END OF THE SCHOOL OF THE COMPANY.

HARDEE'S TACTICS.

VOL. II.

SCHOOL OF THE BATTALION.

RIFLE AND LIGHT INFANTRY TACTICS.

TITLE FOURTH.

SCHOOL OF THE BATTALION.

Formation of the Battalion.

1. Every colonel will labor to habituate his battalion to form line of battle, by night as well as by day, with the greatest possible promtitude.

2. The color-company will generally be designated as the directing company. That, as soon as formed, will be placed on the direction the colonel may have determined for the line of battle. The other companies will form on it, to the right and left, on the principles of successive formations which will be herein prescribed.

3. The color-bearer may have received the color from the hands of the colonel, but if there be daylight, and time, the color will be produced with due solemnity.

Composition and march of the color-escort

4. When the battalion turns out under arms, and the color is wanted, a company, other than that of the color, will be put in march to receive and escort it.

5. The march will be in the following order, in quick time, and without music: the field music, followed by the band; the escort in column by platoon, right in front, with arms on the right shoulder and the color-bearer between the platoons.

6. Arrived in front of the tent or quarters of the colonel, the escort will form line, the field music and band on the right, and arms will be brought to a shoulder.

7. The moment the escort is in line, the color-bearer, preceded by the first lieutenant, and followed by a sergeant of the escort, will go to receive the color.

8. When the color-bearer shall come out, followed by the lieutenant and sergeant, he will halt before the entrance, the escort will present arms, and the field music will sound *to the color*.

9. After some twenty seconds, the captain will cause the sound to cease, arms to be shouldered, and then break by platoon into column; the color-bearer will place himself between the platoons, and the lieutenant and sergeant will resume their posts.

10. The escort will march back to the battalion to the sound of music, in quick time, and in the same order as above: the guide on the right. The march will be so conducted that when the escort

arrives at one hundred and fifty paces in front of the right of the the battalion, the direction of the march will be parallel to its front, and when the color arrives nearly opposite its place in line, the column will change direction to the left, and the right guide will direct himself on the center of the battalion

Honors paid to the color.

11. Arrived at the distance of twenty paces from the battalion, the escort will halt, and the music cease; the colonel will place himself six paces before the center of the battalion, the color-bearer will approach the colonel, by the front, in quick time; when at the distance of ten paces, he will halt, the colonel will cause arms to be presented, and *to the color* to be sounded, which being executed, the color-bearer will take his place in the front rank of the color-guard, and the battalion, by command, shoulder arms.

12. The escort, field music, and band, will return in quick time to their several places in line of battle, marching by the rear of the battalion

13. The color will be escorted back to the colonel's tent or quarters in the above order.

General Rules and Division of the School of the Battalion

14. This school has for its object the instruction of battalions singly, and thus to prepare them for manœuvres in line. The harmony so indispensable in the movements of many battalions, can only be attained by the use of the same commands, the same principles, and the same means of execution. Hence, all colonels, and actual commanders of battalions will conform themselves, without addition or curtailment, to what will herein be prescribed.

15. When a battalion instructed in this drill shall manœuvre in line, the colonel will regulate its movements, as prescribed in the third volume of the Tactics for heavy infantry.

16. The school of the battalion will be divided into five parts.

17. The first will comprehend opening and closing ranks, and the execution of the different fires

18. The second, the different modes of passing from the order in battle, to the order in column

19. The third, the march in column, and the other movements incident thereto

20. The fourth, the different modes of passing from the order in column to the order in battle.

21. The fifth will comprehend the march in line of battle, in advance and in retreat; the passage of defiles in retreat; the march by the flank; the formation by file into line of battle; the change of front; the column doubled on the center; dispositions against cavalry; the rally, and rules for manœuvring by the rear rank.

SCHOOL OF THE BATTALION.

PART FIRST.

Opening and closing ranks, and the execution of the different fires.

ARTICLE I.—*To open and close ranks.*

22. The colonel, wishing the ranks to be opened, will command:

1. *Prepare to open ranks*

23. At this command, the lieutenant-colonel and major will place themselves on the right of the battalion, the first on the flank of the file closers, and the second four paces from the front rank of the battalion.

24. These dispositions being made, the colonel will command

2. *To the rear, open order.* 3. MARCH.

25. At the second command, the covering sergeants, and the sergeant on the left of the battalion, will place themselves four paces in the rear of the front rank, and opposite their places in line of battle, in order to mark the new alignment of the rear rank; they will be aligned by the major on the left sergeant of the battalion, who will be careful to place himself exactly four paces in rear of the front rank, and to hold his piece between the eyes, erect and inverted, the better to indicate to the major the direction to be given to the covering sergeants.

26. At the command *march*, the rear rank and the file closers will step to the rear without counting steps; the men will pass a little in rear of the line traced for this rank, halt, and dress forward on the covering sergeants, who will align correctly the men of their respective companies.

27. The file closers will fall back and preserve the distance of two paces from the rear rank, glancing eyes to the right; the lieutenant-colonel will from the right, align them on the file closer of the left, who, having placed himself accurately two paces from the rear rank, will invert his piece, and hold it up erect between his eyes, the better to be seen by the lieutenant-colonel.

28. The colonel, seeing the ranks aligned, will command.

1. FRONT.

At this command, the lieutenant-colonel, major, and the left sergeant, will retake their places in line of battle.

29. The colonel will cause the ranks to be closed by the commands prescribed for the instructor in the School of the Company, No. 28.

ARTICLE II.—*Manual of Arms.*

30. The ranks being closed, the colonel will cause the following times and pauses to be executed

Present arms.	(then)	*Shoulder arms*
Order arms		*Shoulder arms.*
Support arms		*Shoulder arms*
Fix bayonet	.	*Shoulder arms*
Charge bayonet.	.	*Shoulder arms*
Unfix bayonet		*Shoulder arms*

ARTICLE III.—*Loading at will and the Firings*

31. The colonel will next cause to be executed loading at will, by the commands prescribed in the School of the Company No. 45; the officers and sergeants in the ranks will half face to the right with the men at the eighth time of loading, and will face to the front when the men next to them come to a shoulder.

32. The colonel will cause to be executed the fire by company, the fire by wing, the fire by battalion, the fire by file, and the fire by rank, by the commands to be herein indicated.

33. The fire by company and the fire by file will always be direct; the fire by battalion, the fire by wing, and the fire by rank, may be either direct or oblique.

34. When the fire ought to be oblique, the colonel will give, at every round, the caution *right* (or *left*) *oblique*, between the commands *ready* and *aim*.

35. The fire by company will be executed alternately by the right and left companies of each division, as if the division were alone. The right company will fire first, the captain of the left will not give his first command till he shall see one or two pieces at a ready in the right company, the captain of the latter, after the first discharge, will observe the same rule in respect to the left company, and the fire will thus be continued alternately.

36. The colonel will observe the same rule in the firing by wing.

37. The fire by file will commence in all the companies at once, and will be executed as has been prescribed in the School of the Company No. 55 and following. The fire by rank will be executed by each rank alternately, as has been prescribed in the School of the Company No. 58 and following.

38. The color-guard will not fire, but reserve itself for the defense of the color.

The fire by company.

39. The colonel, wishing the fire by company to be executed, will command:

1. *Fire by company.* 2. *Commence firing.*

40. At the first command, the captains and covering sergeants will take the positions indicated in the school of the company, No. 49.

41. The color and its guard will step back at the same time, so as to bring the front rank of the guard in a line with the rear rank of the battalion. *This rule is general for all the different firings.*

42. At the second command, the odd numbered companies will commence to fire; their captains will each give the commands prescribed in the school of the company, No 50, observing to precede the command *company* by that of *first*, *third*, *fifth*, or *seventh*, according to the number of each.

43. The captains of the even numbered companies will give, in their turn, the same commands, observing to precede them by the number of their respective companies.

44. In order that the odd numbered companies may not all fire at once, their captains will observe, but only for the first discharge, to give the command *fire* one after another, thus, the captain of the third company will not give the command *fire* until he has heard the fire of the first company, the captain of the fifth will observe the same rule with respect to the third, and the captain of the seventh the same rule with respect to the fifth

45 The colonel will cause the fire to cease by the sound to *cease firing*, at this sound, the men will execute what is prescribed in the school of the company, No 63, at the sound, for officers to take their places after firing, the captains, covering sergeants, and color-guard, will promptly resume their places in line of battle · *this rule is general for all the firings*

The fire by wing.

46. When the colonel shall wish this fire to be executed, he will command

1. *Fire by wing.* 2. *Right wing* 3. READY. 4. AIM. 5. FIRE. 6. LOAD.

47 The colonel will cause the wings to fire alternately, and he will recommence the fire by the commands. 1 *Right wing*; 2 AIM, 3. FIRE; 4 LOAD 1 *Left wing*, 2 AIM, 3. FIRE; 4. LOAD, in conforming to what is prescribed No 35

The fire by battalion.

48. The colonel will cause this fire to be executed by the commands last prescribed, substituting for the first two, 1. *Fire by battalion.* 2. *Battalion.*

The fire by file

49 To cause this to be executed, the colonel will command:

1. *Fire by file.* 2. *Battalion* 3 READY. 4. *Commence firing.*

50 At the fourth command, the fire will commence on the right of each company, as prescribed in the school of the company, No. 57. The colonel may, if he thinks proper, cause the fire to commence on the right of each platoon.

The fire by rank

51. To cause this fire to be executed, the colonel will command:

1 *Fire by rank* 2 *Battalion* 3 READY. 4 *Rear rank.* 5. AIM. 6. FIRE. 7 LOAD.

52 This fire will be executed as has been explained in the school of the company, No. 59, in following the progression prescribed for the two ranks which shou'd fire alternately.

To fire by the rear rank

53. When the colonel shall wish the battalion to fire to the rear, he will command ·

1. *Face by the rear rank.* 2. *Battalion* 3. *About*—FACE.

54. At the first command, the captains, covering sergeants, and file closers will execute what has been prescribed in the school of the company, No 69; the color-bearer will pass into the rear rank, and for this purpose, the corporal of his file will step before the corporal next on his right to let the color-bearer pass, and will then take his place in the front rank, the lieutenant colonel, adjutant, major, sergeant major, and the music will place themselves before the front rank, and face to the rear, each opposite his place in the line of battle—the first two passing around the right, and the others around the left of the battalion.

55. At the third command, the battalion will face about, the captains and covering sergeants observing what is prescribed in the school of the company, No. 70.

56. The battalion facing thus by the rear rank, the colonel will cause it to execute the different fires by the same commands as if it were faced by the front rank

57. The right and left wings will retain the same designations, although faced about, the companies also will preserve their former designations, as *first, second, third,* etc

58 The fire by file will commence on the left of each company, now become the right.

59. The fire by rank will commence by the front rank, now become the rear rank This rank will preserve its denomination

60. The captains, covering sergeants, and color-guard will, at the first command given by the colonel, take the places prescribed for them in the fires with the front rank leading

61. The colonel, after firing to the rear, wishing to face the battalion to its proper front, will command :

1. *Face by the front rank* 2 *Battalion.* 3. *About*—FACE

62. At these commands, the battalion will return to its proper front by the means prescribed Nos 54 and 55.

63 The fire by file being that most used in war, the colonel will give it the preference in the preparatory exercises, in order that the battalion may be brought to execute it with the greatest possible regularity.

64 When the colonel may wish to give some relaxation to the battalion, without breaking the ranks, he will execute what has been prescribed in the school of the company, Nos 37 and 38, or Nos 39 and 40

65 When the colonel shall wish to cause arms to be stacked, he will bring the battalion to ordered arms, and then command

1 *Stack*—ARMS 2 *Break ranks.* 3. MARCH

66. The colonel wishing the men to return to the ranks, will cause *attention* to be sounded, at which the battalion will re-form behind the stacks of arms The sound being finished, the colonel, after causing the stacks to be broken, will command

Battalion.

67. At this command, the men will fix their attention, and remain immovable.

PART SECOND

Different modes of passing from the order in battle to the order in column.

ARTICLE I.—*To break to the right or the left into column*

68. Lines of battle will habitually break into column by company; they may also break by division or by platoon.

69. It is here supposed that the colonel wishes to break by company to the right, he will command

1 *By company, right wheel.* 2 MARCH (or *double quick*—MARCH).

70. At the first command, each captain will place himself rapidly before the center of his company, and caution it that it has to wheel to the right, each covering sergeant will replace his captain in the front rank

71 At the command *march*, each captain will break to the right, according to the principles prescribed in the school of the company No. 173; each captain will conform himself to what is prescribed for the chiefs of platoon, the left guide, as soon as he can pass, will place himself on the left of the front rank, to conduct the marching flank, and when he shall have approached near to the perpendicular, the captain will command: 1. *Such company.* 2. HALT

72 At the second command, which will be given at the instant the left guide shall be at the distance of three paces from the perpendicular, the company will halt; the guide will advance and place his left arm lightly against the breast of the captain, who will establish him on the alignment of the man who has faced to the right; the covering sergeant will place himself correctly on the alignment on the right of that man, which being executed, the captain will align his company by the left, command FRONT, and place himself two paces before its center

73 The captains having commanded FRONT, the guides, although some of them may not be in the direction of the preceding guides, will stand fast, in order that the error of a company that has wheeled too much or too little may not be propagated, the guides not in the direction will readily come into it when the column is put in march

74 A battalion in line of battle will break into column by company to the left, according to the same principles, and by inverse means, the covering sergeant of each company will conduct the marching flank, and the left guide will place himself on the left of the front rank at the moment the company halts.

75. When the battalion breaks by division, the indication *division* will be substituted in the commands for that of *company*, the chief of each division (the senior captain) will place himself to

what is prescribed for the chief of company, and will place himself two paces before the center of his division; the junior captain, if not already there, will place himself in the interval between the two companies in the front rank, and be covered by the covering sergeant of the left company in the rear rank. The right guide of the right company will be the right guide, and the left guide of the left company, the left guide of the division.

76. When the battalion shall break by platoon to the right or to the left, each first lieutenant will pass around to the left of his company to place himself in front of the second platoon, and for this purpose, each covering sergeant, except the one of the right company, will step, for the moment, in rear of the right file of his company.

77. When the battalion breaks by division to the right, and there is an odd company, the captain of this company, (the left), after wheeling into column, will cause it to oblique to the left, halt it at company distance from the preceding division, place his left guide on the direction of the column, and then align his company by the left. When the line breaks by division to the left, the odd company will be in front; its captain, having wheeled it into column, will cause it to oblique to the right, halt it at division distance from the division next in the rear, place his right guide on the direction of the other guides, and align the company by the right.

78. The battalion being in column, the lieutenant colonel and major will place themselves on the directing flank, the first abreast with the leading subdivision, and the other abreast with the last, and both six paces from the flank. The adjutant will be near the lieutenant-colonel, and the sergeant-major near the major.

79. The colonel will have no fixed place as the *instructor* of his battalion; but in columns composed of many battalions, he will place himself habitually on the directing flank fifteen or twenty paces from the guides, and abreast with the center of his battalion.

80. When the colonel shall wish to move the column forward without halting it, he will caution the battalion to that effect, and command:

1. *By company, right wheel.* 2. MARCH (or *double quick*—MARCH).

81. At the first command, the captains of companies will execute what is prescribed for breaking into a column from a halt.

82. At the second command, they will remain in front of their companies to superintend the movement; the companies will wheel to the right on fixed pivots as indicated in the School of the Company No. 185; the left guides will conform to what is prescribed above; when they shall arrive near the perpendicular, the colonel will command:

3. *Forward.* 4. MARCH. 5. *Guide left.*

83. At the third command, each covering sergeant will place himself by the right side of the man on the right of the front rank of his company. At the fourth command, which will be given at

the instant the wheel is completed, the companies will cease to wheel and march straight forward. At the fifth, the men will take the touch of elbows to the left. The leading guide will march in the direction indicated to him by the lieutenant-colonel. The guides will immediately conform themselves to the principles of the march in column, School of the Company No. 200, and following.

84. If the battalion be marching in line of battle, the colonel will cause it to wheel to the right or left, by the same commands and the same means; but he should previously caution the battalion that it is to continue the march.

85. A battalion in line of battle will break into column by company to the left, according to the same principles, by inverse means; the covering sergeant of each company will conduct the marching flank, and the left guides will place themselves on the left of their respective companies at the command *forward*.

86. When a battalion has to prolong itself in column towards the right or left, or has to direct its march in column perpendicularly or diagonally in front, or in rear of either flank, the colonel will cause it to break by company to the right or left, as has just been prescribed; but when the line breaks to the right, in order to march towards the left, or the reverse, the colonel will command: *Break to the right to march to the left*, or *break to the left to march to the right*, before giving the command, *by company, right (or left) wheel*. As soon as the battalion is broken, the lieutenant colonel will place a marker abreast with the right guide of the leading company. The instant the column is put in motion, this company will wheel to the left (or right) march ten paces to the front without changing the guide, and wheel again to the left (or right). The second wheel being completed, the captain will immediately command *guide left* (or *right*.) The guide of this company will march in a direction parallel to the guides of the column. The lieutenant-colonel will be careful to place a second marker at the point where the first company is to change direction the second time.

ARTICLE II.—*To break to the rear, by the right or left, into column; and to advance or retire by the right or left of companies.*

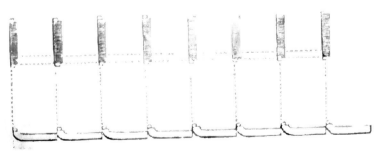

87. When the colonel shall wish to cause the battalion to break to the rear, by the right, into column by company, he will command:

1. *By the right of companies to the rear into column.* 2. *Battalion right*—FACE. 3. MARCH (or *double quick*—MARCH).

88. At the first command, each captain will place himself before the center of his company, and caution it to face to the right; the covering sergeants will step into the front rank.

89. At the second command, the battalion will face to the right; each captain will hasten to the right of the company, and break two files to the rear; the first file will break the whole depth of the two ranks; the second file less; which being executed, the captain will place himself so that his breast may touch lightly the left arm of the front rank man of the last file in the company next on the right of his own. The captain of the right company will place himself as if there were a company on his right, and will align himself on the other captains. The covering sergeant of each company will break to the rear with the right files, and place himself before the front rank of the first file, to conduct him.

90. At the command *march*, the first file of each company will wheel to the right; the covering sergeant, placed before this file, will conduct it perpendicularly to the rear. The other files will come successively to wheel on the same spot. The captains will stand fast, see their companies file past, and at the instant the last file shall have wheeled, each captain will command:

1. *Such company.* 2. HALT. 3. FRONT. 4. *Left*—DRESS.

91. At the instant the company faces to the front, its left guide will place himself so that his left arm may touch lightly the breast of his captain.

92. At the fourth command, the company will align itself on its left guide, the captain so directing it, that the new alignment may be perpendicular to that which the company had occupied in line of battle, and, the better to judge this, he will step back two paces from the flank.

93. The company being aligned, the captain will command: FRONT, and take his place before its center.

94. The battalion marching in line of battle, when the colonel shall wish to break into column by company, to the rear, by the right, he will command:

1. *By the right of companies to the rear into column.* 2. *Battalion, by the right flank.* 3. MARCH (or *double quick*—MARCH).

95. At the first command, each captain will step briskly in front of the center of his company, and caution it to face *by the right flank*.

96. At the command *march*, the battalion will face to the right; each captain will move rapidly to the right of his company, and cause it to break to the right; the first file of each company will

wheel to the right, and the covering sergeant, placed in front of this file, will conduct it perpendicularly to the rear; the other files will wheel successively at the same place as the first. The captains will see their companies file past them, when the last files have wheeled, the colonel will command:

3 *Battalion, by the left flank*—MARCH. 4. *Guide left.*

97. At the command *march*, the companies will face to the left, and march in column in the new direction. The captains will place themselves in front of the centers of their respective companies. At the fourth command, the guides will conform to the principles of the march in column, the leading one will move in the direction indicated to him by the lieutenant-colonel. The men will take the touch of elbows to the left.

98. To break to the rear by the left, the colonel will give the same commands as in the case of breaking to the rear by the right, substituting the indication *left* for that of *right*.

99. The movement will be executed according to the same principles. Each captain will hasten to the left of his company, cause the first two files to break to the rear, and then place his breast against the right file of the company next to the left of his own, in the manner prescribed above.

100. As soon as the two files break to the rear, the left guide of each company will place himself before the front rank man of the headmost file, to conduct him.

101. The instant the companies face to the front, the right guide of each will place himself so that his right arm may lightly touch the breast of his captain.

102. The battalion may be broken by divisions to the rear, by the right or left, in like manner; in this case the indication *divisions* will be substituted, in the first command, for that of *companies*, the chiefs of division will conform themselves to what is prescribed for the chiefs of company. The junior captain in each division will place himself, when the division faces to a flank, by the side of a covering sergeant of the left company, who steps into the front rank.

103. If there be an odd number of companies, and the battalion breaks by division to the rear, whether by the right or left, the captain of the left company will conform to what is prescribed No. 77.

104. This manner of breaking into column being at once the most prompt and regular, will be preferred on actual service, unless there be some particular reason for breaking to the front.

105. If the battalion be in line and at a halt, and the colonel should wish to advance or retire by the right of companies, he will command:

1 *By the right of companies to the front* (or *rear*). 2 *Battalion, right* FACE. 3 MARCH (or *double quick*—MARCH). 4. *Guide right,* (*left* or *center*)

106. At the first ... pidly two

paces in front of the center of his company, and caution it to face to the right, the covering sergeants will replace the captains in the front rank

107 At the second command, the battalion will face to the right, and each captain moving quickly to the right of his company will cause files to break to the front, according to the principles indicated No 89.

108 At the command *march*, each captain, placing himself on the left of his leading guide, will conduct his company perpendicularly to the original line. At the fourth command, the guide of each company will dress to the right, left, or center, according to the indication given, taking care to preserve accurately his distance.

109. If the colonel should wish to move to the front, or rear, by the left of companies, the movement will be executed by the same means and the same commands, substituting *left* for *right*.

110. If the battalion be in march, and the colonel should wish to advance or retire by the right of companies, he will command:

1. *By the right of companies to the front* (or *rear*) 2. *Battalion, by the right flank* 3. MARCH (or *double quick*—MARCH) 4 *Guide right (left)* or *(center);*

111 Which will be executed according to the principles and means prescribed Nos 95 and following, and 106 and following At the first command, the color and general guides will take their places as in column

112. If the colonel should wish to advance or retire by the left of companies, the movement will be executed by the same means and the same commands, substituting *left* for *right*

113 If the battalion be advancing by the right or left of companies, and the colonel should wish to form line to the front, he will command

1. *By companies into line.* 2 MARCH (or *double quick*—MARCH).
3 *Guide center*

114 At the command *march*, briskly repeated by the captains, each company will be formed into line, as prescribed in the school of the company, No 154

115. At the third command, the color and general guides will move rapidly to their places in line, as will be hereinafter prescribed No. 405.

116. If the battalion be retiring by the right or left of companies, and the colonel should wish to form line facing the enemy, he will first cause the companies to face about while marching, and immediately form in line by the commands and means prescribed No 113, and following

SCHOOL OF THE BATTALION. 103

ARTICLE III.—*To ploy the battalion into close column.*

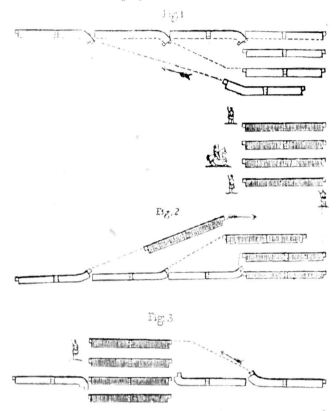

117. This movement may be executed by company or by division, on the right or left subdivision, right or left in front.

118. The examples in this school will suppose the presence of four divisions, with directions for an odd company; but what will be prescribed for four will serve equally for two, three or five divisions.

119. To ploy the battalion into close column by division in rear of the first, the colonel will command:

1. *Close column, by division.* 2. *On the first division, right in front.*
3. *Battalion, right*—FACE. 4. MARCH (or *double quick*—MARCH).

120. At the second command, all the chiefs of division will place themselves before the centers of their divisions; the chief of the first will caution it to stand fast; the chiefs of the three others will remind them that they will have to face to the right, and the covering sergeant of the right company of each division will replace his captain in the front rank, as soon as the latter steps out.

121. At the third command, the last three divisions will face to the right the rest of each division will halt to the right, and

cause files to be broken to the rear, as indicated No 89, the right guide will break at the same time, and place himself before the front rank man of the first file, to conduct him, and each chief of division will place himself by the side of this guide.

122. The moment these divisions face to the right, the junior captain in each will place himself on the left of the covering sergeant of the left company, who will place himself in the front rank. *This rule is general for all the ployments by division.*

123 At the command *march*, the chief of the first division will add, *guide left;* at this, its left guide will place himself on its left, as soon as the movement of the second division may permit, and the file closers will advance one pace upon the rear rank.

124. All the other divisions, each conducted by its chief, will step off together, to take their places in the column; the second will gain, in wheeling by file to the rear, the space of six paces, which ought to separate its guide from the guide of the first division, and so direct its march as to enter the column on a line parallel to this division; the third and fourth divisions will direct themselves diagonally towards, but a little in rear of, the points at which they ought, respectively, to enter the column, at six paces from the left flank of the column, the head of each of these divisions will incline a little to the left, in order to enter the column as has just been prescribed for the second, taking care also to leave the distance of six paces between its guide and the guide of the preceding division At the moment the divisions put themselves in march to enter the column, the file closers of each will incline to the left, so as to bring themselves to the distance of a pace from the rear rank.

125. Each chief of these three divisions will conduct his division till he shall be up with the guide of the directing one, the chief will then himself halt, see his division file pass, and halt it the instant the last file shall have passed, commanding 1 *Such division;* 2. HALT; 3 FRONT; 4 *Left*—DRESS.

126. At the second command, the division will halt; the left guide will place himself promptly on the direction, six paces from the guide which precedes him, in order that, the column being formed, the divisions may be separated the distance of four paces.

127. At the third command, the division will face to the front; at the fourth, it will be aligned by its chief, who will place himself two paces outside of his guide, and direct the alignment so that his division may be parallel to that which precedes—which being done, he will command, FRONT, and place himself before the center of his division.

128 If any division, after the command *front*, be not at its proper distance, and this can only happen through the negligence of its chief, such division will remain in its place, in order that the fault may not be propagated

129 The colonel will superintend the execution of the movement, and cause the prescribed principles to be observed.

130. The lieutenant-colonel, placing himself in succession in rear of the left guides, will assure them on the direction as they arrive, and then move to his place outside of the left flank of the column six paces from, and abreast with, the first division. In assuming the guides on the direction, he will be a mere observer, unless one or more should fail to cover exactly the guide or guides already established. *This rule is general.*

131. The major will follow the movement abreast with the left of the fourth division, and afterwards take his position outside of the left flank of the column, six paces from, and abreast with, this division.

132. To ploy the battalion in front of the first division, the colonel will give the same commands, substituting the indication *left* for that of *right* in front.

133. At the second and third commands, the chiefs of division and the junior captains will conform themselves to what is prescribed, Nos. 120, 121, 122; but the chiefs of the last three divisions, instead of causing the first two files to break to the rear, will cause them to break to the front.

134. At the fourth command, the chief of the first division will add: *Guide right.*

135. The three other divisions will step off together to take their places in the column in front of the directing division; each will direct itself as prescribed, No. 124, and will enter in such manner that, when halted, its guide may find himself six paces from the guide of the division next previously established in the column.

136. Each chief of these divisions will conduct his division, till his right guide shall be nearly up with the guide of the directing one; he will then halt his division, and cause it to face to the front; at the instant it halts, its right guide will face to the rear, place himself six paces from the preceding guide, and cover him exactly—which being done, the chief will align his division by the right.

137. The lieutenant-colonel, placed in front of the right guide of the first division, will assure the guides on the direction as they successively arrive, and then move outside of the right flank of the column, to a point six paces from, and abreast with, the fourth division, now in front.

138. The major will conform himself to what is prescribed, No. 131, and then move outside of the right flank of the column, six paces from, and abreast with, the first division, now in the rear.

139. The movement being ended, the colonel will command:

Guides, about—FACE.

140. At this, the guides, who are faced to the rear, will face to the front.

141. To ploy the battalion in rear, or in front of the fourth division, the colonel will command:

1 *Close column by division* 2 *On the fourth division, left (or right) in front* 3 *Battalion, left*—FACE. 4 MARCH. (or *double quick*—MARCH)

142 These movements will be executed according to the principles of those which precede, but by inverse means the fourth division on which the battalion ploys will stand fast, the instant the movement commences, its chief will command, *guide right (or left).*

143. The foregoing examples embrace all the principles thus, when the colonel shall wish to ploy the battalion on an interior division, he will command:

1. *Close column by division* 2 *On such division, right (or left) in front* 3 *Battalion inwards*—FACE 4 MARCH (or *double quick*—MARCH).

144 The instant the movement commences, the chief of the directing division will command, *guide left (or right).*

145. The divisions which, in the order in battle, are to the right of the directing division, will face to the left, those which are to the left, will face to the right.

146. If the right is to be in front, the right divisions will ploy in front of the directing division, and the left in its rear; the reverse, if the left is to be in front. And in all the foregoing suppositions, the division or divisions contiguous to the directing one, in wheeling by file to the front or rear, will gain the space of six paces, which ought to separate their guides from the guide of the directing division

147. In all the ployments on an interior division, the lieutenant-colonel will assure the positions of the guides in front, and the major those in rear of the directing division

148 If the battalion be in march, instead of at a halt, the movement will be executed by combining the two gaits of quick and double quick time, and always in rear of one of the flank divisions.

149 The battalion being in march, to ploy it in rear of the first division, the colonel will command.

1. *Close column by division* 2. *On the first division.* 3 *Battalion—by the right flank* 4 *Double quick*—MARCH

150 At the second command, each chief of division will move rapidly before the center of his division and caution it to face to the right.

151. The chief of the first division will caution it to continue to march to the front, and he will command *Quick march.*

152. At the command *march*, the chief of the first division will command *Guide left.* At this, the left guide will move to the left flank of the division and direct himself on the point indicated

153 The three other divisions will face to the right and move off in double quick time, breaking to the right to take their places in

column, each chief of division will move rapidly to the right of his division in order to conduct it. The files will be careful to preserve their distances and to march with a uniform and decided step. The color-bearer and general guides will retake their places in the ranks.

154. The second division will immediately enter the column, marching parallel to the first division; its chief will allow it to file past him, and when the last file is abreast of him, will command 1 *Second division, by the left flank*—MARCH. 2 *Guide left*, and place himself in front of the center of his division.

155. At the command *march*, the division will face to the left, at the second command, the left guide will march in the trace of of the left guide of the first division; the men will take the touch of elbows to the left. When the second division has closed to its proper distance, its chief will command *Quick time*—MARCH. This division will then change its step to quick time.

156. The chiefs of the third and fourth divisions will execute their movements according to the same principles, taking care to gain as much ground as possible toward the head of the column.

157. If the battalion has been previously marching in line at double quick time, when the fourth division shall have gained its distance, the colonel will command *Double quick*—MARCH.

158. In this movement, the lieutenant-colonel will move rapidly to the side of the leading guide, give him a point of direction, and then follow the movements of the first division. The major will follow the movement abreast with the left of the fourth division.

Remarks on ploying the Battalion into column.

159. The battalion may be ployed into column at full, or half distance, on the same principles, and by the same commands, substituting for the first command *Column at full (or half) distance, by division*.

160. In the ployments and movements in column, when the subdivisions execute the movements successively, such as—to take or close distances, to change direction by the flank of subdivisions, each chief of subdivision will cause his men to support arms after having aligned it and commanded, FRONT.

PART THIRD.

Article I.—*To march in column at full distance.*

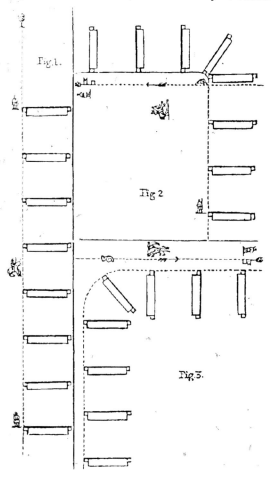

161. When the colonel shall wish to put the column in march, he will indicate to the leading guide two distinct objects in front on the line which the guide ought to follow. This guide will immediately put his shoulders in a square with that line, take the more distant object as the point of direction, and the nearer one as the intermediate point.

162. If only a single prominent object present itself in the direction the guide has to follow, he will face to it as before, and immediately endeavor to catch on the ground some intermediate point, by which to give steadiness to his march on the point of direction.

163. There being no prominent object to serve as the point of direction, the colonel will dispatch the lieutenant-colonel or adju-

tant to place himself forty paces in advance, facing the column, and by a sign of the sword establish him on the direction he may wish to give to the leading guide; that officer being thus placed, this guide will take him as the point of direction, conforming himself to what is prescribed in the school of the company, No. 87.

164. These dispositions being made, the colonel will command

1. *Column forward* 2. *Guide left* (or *right*.) 3. MARCH, (or *double quick*—MARCH.)

165. At the command *march*, briskly repeated by the chiefs of subdivision, the column will put itself in march, conforming to what is prescribed in the school of the company No. 200 and following.

166. The leading guide may always maintain himself correctly on the direction by keeping steadily in view the two points indicated to him, or chosen by himself; if these points have a certain elevation, he may be assured he is on the true direction, when the nearer masks the more distant point.

167. The following guides will preserve with exactness both step and distance; each will march in the trace of the guide who immediately precedes him, without occupying himself with the general direction.

168. The lieutenant-colonel will hold himself, habitually, abreast with the leading guide, to see that he does not deviate from the direction, and will observe, also, that the next guide marches exactly in the trace of the first.

169. The major will generally be abreast with the last subdivision; he will see that each guide marches exactly in the trace of the one immediately preceding; if either deviate from the direction, the major will promptly rectify the error, and prevent its being propagated; but he need not interfere, in this way, unless the deviation has become sensible, or material.

170. The column being in march, the colonel will frequently cause the *about* to be executed while marching; to this effect, he will command

1. *Battalion, right about* 2. MARCH 3. *Guide right.*

171. At the second command, the companies will face to the right about, and the column will then march forward in an opposite direction; the chiefs of subdivision will remain behind the front rank, the file closers in front of the rear rank, and the guides will place themselves in the same rank. The lieutenant-colonel will remain abreast of the first division, now in rear; the major will give a point of direction to the leading guide, and march abreast of him.

172. The colonel will hold himself habitually on the directing flank; he will look to the step and to the distances, and see that all the principles prescribed for the march in column, school of the company, are observed.

173. These means, which the practice in that school ought to have rendered familiar, will give sufficient exactness to the direc-

tion of the column, and also enable it to form *forward* or *faced to the rear, on the right*, or *on the left*, into line of battle, and *to close in mass.*

174. But when a column, arriving in front, or in rear of the line of battle, or, rather, on one of the extremities of that line, has to prolong itself on it, in order to form *to the left* or *to the right* into line of battle, then, as it is essential, to prevent the columns from cutting the line, or sensibly deviating from it, other means, as follows, will be employed

The column arriving in front of the line of battle, to prolong it on this line.

175 If the column right in front arrive in front of the line of battle, as it should cross it and find itself four paces beyond it, after having changed direction, the colonel will cause to be placed, in advance, a marker on the line to indicate the point at which the column ought to cross it, and another marker to indicate the point where the first subdivision should commence to wheel, he will be so placed that when the wheel is executed, the left guide will find himself four paces within the line of battle. The chief of the leading subdivision, when the head of the column shall have arrived near the line, will take the guide to the right, and this guide will immediately direct himself on the second marker On arriving abreast of him, this subdivision will be wheeled to the left, and when the wheel is completed, the guide will be changed again to the left, this guide will then march parallel to the line of battle by the means to be hereinafter indicated.

176. The instant the first subdivision wheels, the right general guide, who, by a caution from the lieutenant-colonel, will before have placed himself on the line of battle at the point where the column crosses it, and who will have faced to the two points of direction in his front, indicated by the colonel, will march forward correctly on the prolongation of those points

177 The color-bearer will place himself in like manner on the line of battle, and, at the instant the color subdivision wheels, he will prolong his march on that line, abreast with this subdivision, taking care to carry the color lance before the center of his person, and to maintain himself exactly in the direction of the general guide who precedes him, and the point of direction in front which will have been indicated to him

178 Finally, the left guide will place himself in the same manner on the line of battle, and, at the instant the last subdivision of the battalion wheels, he will march correctly in the direction of the color-bearer and the other general guide.

179. The guide of the first subdivision will march steadily abreast with the right general guide, and about four paces to his right, each of the guides of the following subdivisions will march, in the trace of the guide who immediately precedes him, as prescribed, No. 167

180. The colonel, placed outside of the general guides, will see that the column marches nearly parallel to, and about four paces within these guides

181. The lieutenant-colonel and major will look to the direction of the general guides, and to this end, place themselves sometimes in rear of the color-bearer, or the left general guide

182. If the column be composed of several battalions, the general guides of each will successively place themselves on the line of battle to prolong their march on this line, as the leading subdivision, that of the color, and the one in the rear of their battalion, shall wheel into the new direction, these guides will conform themselves respectively, as will also the colonel, lieutenant-colonel and major, to what is prescribed above for those of the leading battalion

183. In the case of several battalions, the lieutenant-colonel of each will maintain steadily the guide of his leading subdivision about four paces within the line of general guides, even should the last subdivisions of the battalion immediately preceding deviate from the parallelism, in order that the false direction of one battalion may not influence that of the battalions which follow

The column arriving behind the line of battle, to prolong it on this line

184. If the column, right in front, arrive behind the line of battle, as it ought to find itself four paces within this line, after having changed direction, the colonel will cause a marker to be placed at the point where, according to that condition, the first subdivision ought to commence wheeling Another marker will be established on the line of battle, to indicate the point at which the general guides ought, in succession, to begin to prolong themselves on that line; he will be so placed that each subdivision, having finished its wheel, may find itself nearly in a line with this marker

185. At the instant the first subdivision, after having wheeled to the right, begins to prolong itself parallelly to the line of battle, the leading general guide, placed in advance on that line, will direct himself on the two points taken in his front; the color-bearer and the other general guide will successively place themselves on the same line the instant that their respective subdivisions shall have finished their wheel

186. If the column be composed of several battalions, the general guides of the following battalions will successively execute what has been just prescribed for those of the leading battalion, and the whole will conform themselves, as well as the guides of subdivisions, and the field officers of the several battalions, to what is indicated above for a column arriving in front of the line of battle.

187. In a column, left in front, arriving in front or in rear of the line of battle, these movements will be executed on the same principles, and by inverse means

The column arriving on the right or the left of the line of battle, to prolong it on this line.

188. If the column, instead of arriving in front or in rear of the line of battle, arrive on its right or left, and if it have to prolong itself on that line, in order afterwards to form to the left or right into line of battle, the colonel will bring the color and general guides on the flank of the column by the command *color and general guides on the line;* and these guides will prolong themselves on the line of battle, conforming to what is prescribed above.

ARTICLE III.—*To change direction in column at full distance.*

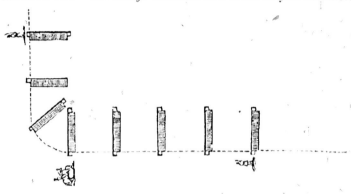

231. The column being in march in the cadenced step, when the colonel shall wish to cause it to change direction, he will go to the point at which the change ought to be commenced, and establish a marker there, presenting the breast to the flank of the column; this marker, no matter to which side the change of direction is to be made, will be posted on the opposite side, and he will remain in position till the last subdivision of the battalion shall have passed. The leading subdivision being within a few paces of the marker, the colonel will command:

Head of column to the left (or *right*).

232. At this, the chief of the leading subdivision will immediately take the guide on the side opposite the change of direction, if not already there. This guide will direct himself so as to graze the breast of the marker; arrived at this point, the chief will cause his subdivision to change direction by the commands and according to the principles prescribed in the School of the Company. When the wheel is completed, the chief of this subdivision will retake the guide, if changed, on the side of the primitive direction.

233. The chief of each succeeding subdivision, as well as the guides, will conform to what has just been explained for the leading subdivision.

235. The colonel will carefully see that the guide of each subdivision, in wheeling, does not throw himself without or within, but

passes over all the points of the arc of the circle, which he ought to describe

235. As often as no distinct object presents itself in the new direction, the lieutenant-colonel will place himself upon it in advance, at the distance of thirty or forty paces from the marker, and be assured in this direction by the colonel; the leading guide will take, the moment he shall have changed direction, two points on the ground in the straight line which, drawn from himself, would pass between the heels of the lieutenant-colonel, taking, afterwards, new points as he advances

236. The major will see that the guides direct themselves on the marker, posted at the point of change, so as to graze his breast.

237. If the column be composed of several battalions, the lieutenant-colonel of the second, will cause the marker of the first battalion, to be replaced as soon as the last subdivision of this battalion shall have passed; this disposition will be observed by battalion after battalion, to the rear of the column.

ARTICLE IV.—*To halt the column*

239. The column being in march, when the colonel shall wish to halt it, he will command

1. *Column* 2. HALT

240. At the second command, briskly repeated by the captains, the column will halt, no guide will stir, though he may have lost his distance, or be out of the direction of the preceding guides.

241. The column being in march, in double quick time, will be halted by the same commands. At the command *halt*, the men will halt in their places, and will themselves rectify their positions in the ranks

242. The column being halted, when the colonel shall wish to form it into line of battle, he will move a little in front of the leading guide, and face to him; this guide and the following one will fix their eyes on the colonel, in order promptly to conform themselves to his directions

243. If the colonel judge it not necessary to give a general direction to the guides, he will limit himself to rectifying the position of such as may be without, or within the direction, by the command *guide of (such) company, or guides of (such) companies, to the right, (or to the left;)* at this command, the guides designated will place themselves on the direction; the others will stand fast

244. If, on the contrary, the colonel judge it necessary to give a general direction to the guides of the column, he will place the first two on the direction he shall have chosen, and command:

Guides, cover.

245. At this, the following guides will promptly place themselves on the direction covering the first two in file, and each precisely at a distance equal to the front of his company, from the guide immediately preceding; the lieutenant-colonel will assure them in the direction

Left (or *right*)—DRESS.

248. At this command, the guide of each company of the directing flank will step promptly into the direction of the general guides, and face to the front. The lieutenant-colonel, placed in front of, and facing to, the leading general guide, and the major, placed in rear of the rearmost one, will promptly align the company guides.

249. The colonel, having verified the direction of the guides, will command:

Left (or *right*)—DRESS.

250. This will be executed as prescribed, No. 246.

ARTICLE V.—*To close the column to half distance, or in mass.*

252. A column by company being at full distance right in front, and at a halt, when the colonel shall wish to cause it to close to half distance, on the leading company, he will command:

1. *To half distance, close column.* 2. MARCH (or *double quick—MARCH*)

253. At the first command, the captain of the leading company will caution it to stand fast.

254. At the command *march*, which will be repeated by all the captains, except the captain of the leading company, this company will stand fast, and its chief will align it by the left; the file closers will close one pace upon the rear rank.

255. All the other companies will continue to march, and as each in succession arrives at platoon distance from the one which precedes, its captain will halt it.

256. At the instant that each company halts, its guide will place himself on the direction of the guides who precede, and the captain will align the company by the left; the file closers will close one pace upon the rear rank.

257. No particular attention need be given to the general direction of the guides before they respectively halt, it will suffice if each follow in the trace of the one who precedes him.

258. The colonel, on the side of the guides, will superintend the execution of the movement, observing that the captains halt their companies exactly at platoon distance the one from the other.

259. The lieutenant-colonel, a few paces in front, will face to the leading guide and assure the positions of the following guides as they successively place themselves on the direction.

260. The major will follow the movement abreast with the last guide.

261. If the column be in march, the colonel will cause it to close by the same commands.

262. If the column be marching in double quick time, at the first command, the captain of the leading company will command *quick time*, the chiefs of the other companies will caution them to continue their march.

SCHOOL OF THE BATTALOIN.   115

263. At the command *march*, the leading company will march in quick, and the other companies in double quick time; and as each arrives at platoon distance from the preceding one, its chief will cause it to march in quick time.

264. When the rearmost company shall have gained its distance, the colonel will command:

Double quick—MARCH.

To close the column on the eighth, or rearmost company.

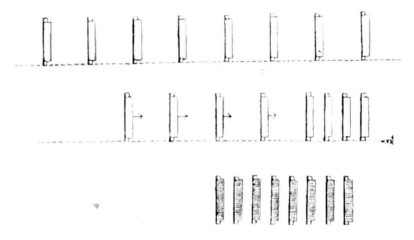

267. The column being at a halt, if instead of causing it to close to half distance on the first company, the colonel should wish to cause it to close on the eighth, he will command:

1. *On the eighth company, to half distance close column.* 2. *Battalion, about*—FACE. 3. *Column forward.* 4. *Guide right.* 5. MARCH (or *double quick*—MARCH).

268. At the second command, all the companies, except the eighth, will face about, and their guides will remain in the front rank, now the rear.

269. At the fourth command, all the captains will place themselves two paces outside of their companies on the directing flank.

270. At the command *march*, the eighth company will stand fast, and its captain will align it by the left, the other companies will put themselves in march, and, as each arrives at platoon distance from the one established before it, its captain will halt it and face it to the front. At the moment that each company halts, the left guide, remaining faced to the rear, will place himself promptly on the direction of the guides already established. Immediately after the captain will align his company by the left, and the file closers will close one pace on the rear rank. If this movement be executed in double quick time, the captains, at the second command

mand *Such company, right about*—HALT At this command, the company designated will face to the right about and halt.

271. All the companies being aligned, the colonel will cause the guides, who stand faced to the rear, to face about.

272. The lieutenant-colonel, placing himself behind the rearmost guide, will assure successively the positions of the other guides as prescribed No 259, the major will remain abreast with the rearmost company

273 The column being in march, when the colonel shall wish to close it on the eighth company, he will command

1. *On the eighth company, to half distance, close column.* 2 *Battalion right about.* 3. MARCH (or *double quick*—MARCH). 4 *Guide right.*

274. At the first command, the captain of the eighth company will caution his company that it will remain faced to the front, the captains of the other companies will caution their companies that they will have to face about

275 At the command *march*, the captain of the eighth company will halt his company and align it by the left, the file closers will close one pace upon the rear rank

276. The captains of the other companies, at the same command, will place themselves on the flank of the column, the subdivisions will face about, and as each arrives at platoon distance from the company immediately preceding it, its chief will face it to the front and halt it as prescribed No 270. The instant each company halts, the guide on the directing flank, remaining faced to the rear, will quickly place himself on the direction of the guides already established. After which, the captain will align the company by the left, and the file closers will close one pace upon the rear rank.

277. The lieutenant-colonel will follow the movement abreast of the first company The major will place himself a few paces in rear of the guide of the eighth company, and will assure successively the position of the other guides.

ARTICLE VI —*To march in column at half distance, or closed in mass.*

281. A column at half distance or in mass, being at a halt, the colonel will put it in march by the commands prescribed for a column at full distance

282 The means of direction will also be the same for a column at half distance or in mass, as for a column at full distance, except that the general guides will not step out.

283 A column, at half distance or in mass, being in march, when the colonel shall wish to halt it, he will give the commands prescribed for halting a column at full distance, and if, afterwards, he judge it necessary to give a general direction to the guides of the column, he will employ, to this end, the commands and means indicated No. 244, and following

284. In columns at half distance or closed in mass, chiefs of sub-

divisions will repeat the commands *march* and *halt*, as in columns at full distance.

285. The colonel will often march the column to the rear, by the means and the commands prescribed Nos. 170 and 171.

286 A column, by division or company, whether at full or half distance or closed in mass, at a halt or marching, can be faced to the right or left, and marched off in the new direction.

ARTICLE VII.—*To change direction in column ot half distance*

287. A column at half distance, being in march, will change direction by the same commands and according to the same principles as a column at full distance; but as the distance between the subdivisions is less, the pivot man in each subdivision will take steps of fourteen inches instead of nine, and of seventeen inches instead of eleven according to the gait, in order to clear, in time, the wheeling point, and the marching flank will describe the arc of a larger circle, the better to facilitate the movement.

ARTICLE VIII.—*To change direction in column closed in mass*

1st *To change direction in marching.*

288 A column by division, closed in mass, being in march, will change direction by the *front* of subdivisions.

289. Whether the change be made to the reverse, or to the pivot flank, it will always be executed on the principle of wheeling in marching; to this end, the colonel will firscause the battalion to take the guide on the flank opposite to the intended change of direction, if it be not already on that flank.

290 A column by division, closed in mass, right in front, having to change direction to the right, the colonel, after having caused a marker to be placed at the point where the change ought to commence, will command

118   SCHOOL OF THE BATTALION.

1. *Battalion, right wheel.*   2. MARCH.

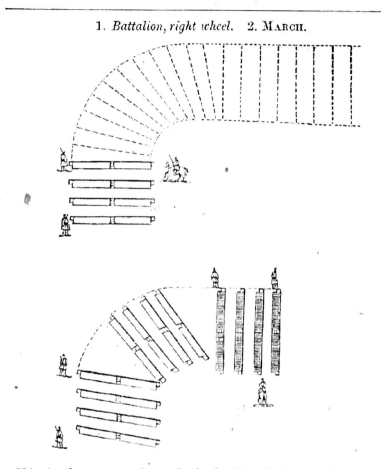

291. At the command *march*, the leading division will wheel as if it were part of a column at half distance.

292. The instant that this division commences the wheel, all the others will, at once, conform themselves to its movement; to this end, the left guide of each, advancing slightly the left shoulder, and lengthening a little the step, will incline to the left, and will observe, at the same time, to gain so much ground to the front that there may constantly be an interval of four paces between his division and that which precedes it; and as soon as he shall cover the preceding guide, he will cease to incline and then march exactly in his trace.

293. Each division will conform itself to the movement of its guide; the men will feel lightly the elbow toward him and advance a little the left shoulder the instant the movement commences; each file, in inclining, will gain so much the less ground to the front, as the file shall be nearer to the pivot, and the right guide will gain only so much as may be necessary to maintain between his

SCHOOL OF THE BATTALION.

own and the preceding division the same distance which separates their marching flanks.

294. Each chief of division, turning to it, will regulate its march, and see that it remains constantly included between its guides; that its alignment continues nearly parallel to that of the preceding division, and that the center bends only a little to the rear.

295. The colonel will superintend the movement, and cause the pivot of the leading division to lengthen or to shorten the step, conforming to the principle established, school of the company, No. 227—if either be necessary to facilitate the movement of the other divisions.

296. The lieutenant-colonel, placed near the left guide of the leading division, will regulate his march, and take care, above all, that he does not throw himself *within* the arc he ought to describe

297. The major, placed in the rear of the guides, will see that the last three conform themselves, each by slight degrees, to the movement of the guide immediately preceding, and that neither inclines too much in the endeavor to cover too promptly the guide in his front. he will rectify any serious fault that may be committed in either of those particulars

298. The colonel, seeing the wheel nearly ended, will command

1. *Forward.* 2. MARCH.

299. At the second command, which will be given at the instant the leading division completes its wheel, it will resume the direct march; the other divisions will conform themselves to this movement; and if any guide find himself not covering his immediate leader, he will, by slight degrees, bring himself on the trace of that guide, by advancing the right shoulder.

300. If the column, right in front, has to change direction to the left, the colonel will first cause it to take the guide to the right, and then command:

1. *Battalion, left wheel.* 2. MARCH

301. At the command *march*, the battalion will change direction to the left, according to the principles just prescribed, and by inverse means

302. When the battalion shall have resumed the direct march, the colonel will change the guide to the left, on seeing the last three guides nearly in the direction of the one in front

303. The foregoing changes in direction will be executed according to the same principles in a column, left in front

304. A column by company, closed in mass, will change direction in marching, by the commands and means indicated for a column by division

305. The guide who is the pivot of the particular wheel, ought to maintain himself at his usual distance of six paces from the guide who precedes him; if this distance be not exactly preserved the divisions would necessarily become confounded, which must be carefully

2d. To change direction from a halt.

306. A column by company, or by division, closed in mass, being at a halt, when the colonel shall wish to give it a new direction, and in which it is to remain, he will cause it to execute this movement by the flanks of subdivisions, in the following manner:

307. The battalion having the right in front, when the colonel shall wish to cause it to change direction by the right flank, he will indicate to the lieutenant-colonel the point of direction to the right; this officer will immediately establish on the new direction two markers, distant from each other a little less than the front of the right file of this subdivision; which being executed, he will command:

1. *Change direction by the right flank.* 2. *Battalion. right*—FACE. 3. MARCH (or *double quick*—MARCH.)

308. At the second command, the column will face to the right, and each chief of subdivision will place himself by the side of his right guide.

309. At the command *march*, all the subdivisions will step off together; the right guide of the leading one will direct himself from the first step, parallelly to the markers placed in advance on the new direction; the chief of the subdivision will not follow the movement, but see it file past, and as soon as the left guide shall have passed, he will command:

1. *First company* (or *first division.*) 2. HALT. 3. FRONT. 4. *Left*—DRESS.

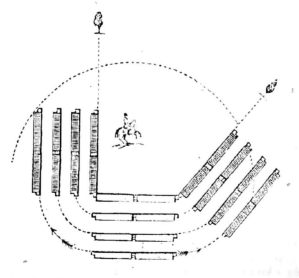

310. At the fourth command, the subdivision will place itself against the two markers, and be promptly aligned by its chief.

311. The right guide of each of the following subdivisions will conform himself to the direction of the right guide of the subdivision preceding his own in the column, so as to enter on the new direction parallelly to that subdivision, and at the distance of four paces from its rear rank.

312. Each chief of subdivision will halt in his own person, on arriving opposite to the left guides already placed on the new direction, see his subdivision file past, and conform himself, in halting and aligning it to what is prescribed No 309.

313. If the change of direction be by the left flank, the colonel will cause markers to be established as before, the first in front of the left file of the leading subdivision, and then give the same commands, substituting the indication *left* for *right*.

314. At the second command all the subdivisions will face to the left, and each chief will place himself by the side of his left guide.

315. At the command *march*, all the subdivisions will step off together, each conducted by its chief.

316. The guide of the leading subdivision will direct himself, from the first step, parallelly to the markers, the subdivision will be conducted by its chief; and as soon as its left guide shall have passed the second marker, it will be halted and aligned as prescribed above, and so of each of the following subdivisions.

317. The colonel will hold himself on the designated flank, to see that each subdivision enters the new direction parallelly to the leading one, and at the prescribed distance from that which precedes.

318. The lieutenant-colonel will place himself in front of, and facing to, the guide of the leading subdivision, and will assure the positions of the following guides, as they successively arrive on the new direction.

319. The major will follow the movement abreast with the last subdivision.

320. In order that this movement may be executed with facility and precision, it is necessary that the leading subdivision should entirely unmask the column, for example, the movement being made by the right flank, it is necessary, before halting the leading subdivision, that its left guide, shall, at least, have arrived at the place previously occupied by its right guide, in order that each following subdivision which has to pass over a space at least equal to its front to put itself in the new direction, and whose left ought to pass the point at which the right had rested, may, at the command *halt*, find itself, in its whole front parallel to the leading subdivision.

321. By this method there is no direction that may not be given to a column in mass.

ARTICLE IX.—*Being in column at half distance, or closed in mass, to take distances.*

322. A column at half distance will take full distances *by the head of* t[he]

tle. If, on the contrary, it has to form itself in line of battle on the ground it occupies, it will take distances *on* the leading or *on* the rearmost subdivision, according as the one or other may find itself at the point where the right or left of the battalion ought to rest in line of battle

1st *To take distances by the head of the column.*

323. The column being by company at half distance and at a halt, when the colonel shall wish to cause it to take full distances by the head, he will command.

By the head of column, take wheeling distance

324. At this command the captain of the leading company will put it on march; to this end, he will command.

1 *First company, forward* 2. *Guide left.* 3 March (or *double quick*—March)

325 When the second shall have nearly its wheeling distance, its captain will command.

1. *Second company, forward.* 2 *Guide left* 3. March (or *double quick*—March)

326. At the command, *march,* which will be pronounced at the instant that this company shall have its wheeling distance, it will step off smartly, taking the step from the preceding company. Each of the other companies will successively execute what has just been prescribed for the second

327 The colonel will see that each company puts itself in march at the instant it has its distance

328 The lieutenant-colonel will hold himself at the head of the column, and direct the march of the leading guide

329. The major will hold himself abreast with the rearmost guide

330. If the column, instead of being at a halt, be in march, the colonel will give the same commands, and add

March (or *double quick*—March)

331 If the column be marching in quick time, at the command *march,* the captain of the leading company will cause *double quick time* to be taken, which will also be done by the other captains as the companies successively attain their proper wheeling distance

232. If the column be marching in *double quick time,* the leading company will continue to march at the same gait. The captains of the other companies will cause *quick time* to be taken, and as each company gains its proper distance its captain will cause it to retake the *double quick step.*

2d *To take distances on the rear of the column.*

333 If the colonel wish to take distances on the rearmost company, he will establish two markers on the direction he shall wish to give to the line of battle, the first opposite to the rearmost com-

pany, the second marker towards the head of the column, at company distance from the first, and both facing to the rear; at the same time, the right general guide, on an intimation from the lieutenant-colonel, will move rapidly a little beyond the point to which the head of the column will extend, and place himself correctly on the prolongation of the two markers. These dispositions being made, the colonel will command:

1. *On the eighth company, take wheeling distance.* 2. *Column forward.* 3. *Guide left.* 4. MARCH (or *double quick*—MARCH.)

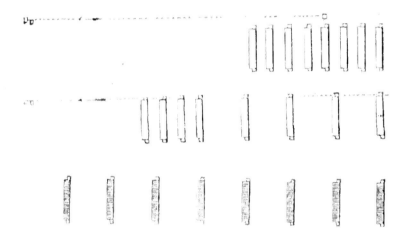

334. At the third command, the captains will place themselves two paces outside of the directing flank; the captain of the eighth company will caution it to stand fast.

335. At the command *march*, repeated by all the captains, except the captain of the eighth company, this latter company will stand fast; its chief will align it on the left by the first marker, who is opposite to this company, and place himself before its center, after commanding *Front*. At this command the marker will retire, and the left guide will take his place.

336. All the other companies will put themselves in march, the guide of the leading one directing himself a little within the right general guide; when the seventh company has arrived opposite the second marker, its captain will halt, and align it on this marker, in the manner prescribed for the eighth company.

337. When the captain of the sixth company shall see that there is, between his company and the seventh, the necessary space for wheeling into line, he will halt his company; the guide facing to the rear will place himself promptly on the direction, and the moment he shall be assured in his position, the captain will align the company by the left, and then place himself two paces before

its center, the other companies will successively conform themselves to what has just been prescribed for the sixth company.

338. The colonel will follow the movement, and see that each company halts at the prescribed distance, he will promptly remedy any fault that may be committed; and, as soon as all the companies shall be aligned, he will cause the guides, who are faced to the rear, to face about

339. The lieutenant-colonel will successively assure the left guides on the direction, placing himself in their rear, as they arrive

340. The major will hold himself at the head of the column, and will direct the march of the leading guide

3d *To take distances on the head of the column.*

341. The colonel, wishing to take distances on the leading company, will establish two markers in the manner just prescribed, one abreast with this company, and the other at company distance in rear of the first, but both facing to the front; the left general guide, on an intimation from the lieutenant-colonel, will move rapidly to the rear, and place himself correctly on the prolongation of the two markers, a little beyond the point to which the rear of the column will extend; these dispositions being made, the colonel will command·

1. *On the first company, take wheeling distance* 2. *Battalion, about*— FACE. 3. *Column, forward* 4 *Guide right* 5. MARCH (or *double quick*—MARCH)

342 At the second command, all the companies, except the one designated, will face about, the guides remaining in the front rank now become the rear

343. At the fourth command, the captains will place themselves outside of their guides

344 At the command *march*, the captain of the designated company will align it, as prescribed, No 335, on the marker placed by its side

345. The remaining companies will put themselves in march, the guide of the rearmost one will direct himself a little within the left general guide, when the second company shall have arrived opposite the second marker, its captain will face it about, conforming to what is prescribed, No 270, and align it, as has just been prescribed for the first company

346 The instant that the third company shall have its wheeling distance, its captain will halt it, facing it about, as prescribed, No 270, and align it by the left, the captains of the remaining companies will each, in succession, conform himself to what has just been prescribed for the captain of the third.

347. The colonel will follow the movement, as indicated No. 338; the lieutenant-colonel and major will conform themselves to what is prescribed, Nos 339 and 340

348. These various movements will be executed according to the same principles in a column with the left in front.

349. They will be executed in like manner in a column closed in mass; but, if it be the wish of the colonel to open out the column to half, instead of full distance, he will substitute, in the commands, the indication *half*, for that of *wheeling* distance.

350. In a column by division, distances will be taken according to the same principles.

ARTICLE X.—*Countermarch of a column at full or half distance.*

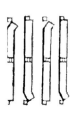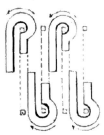

351. In a column at full or half distance, the countermarch will be executed by the means indicated, School of the Company; to this end, the colonel will command:

1. *Countermarch.* 2. *Battalion right* (or *left*)—FACE. 3. *By file left* (or *right*). 4. MARCH (or *double quick*—MARCH).

To countermarch a column closed in mass.

352. If the column be closed in mass, the countermarch will be executed by the commands and means subjoined.

353. The column being supposed formed by division, right in front, the colonel will command:

1. *Countermarch.* 2. *Battalion, right and left*—FACE. 3. *By file left and right.* 4. MARCH (or *double quick*—MARCH).

354. At the first command, the chiefs of the odd numbered divisions will caution them to face the right, and the chiefs of the others to face to the left.

355. At the second command, the odd divisions will face to the right, and the even to the left; the right and left guides of all the divisions will face about; the chiefs of odd divisions will hasten to their right and cause two files to break to the rear, and each chief place himself on the left of the leading front rank man of his division; the chiefs of even divisions will hasten to their left, and cause two files to break to the rear, and each chief place himself on the right of his leading front rank man.

356. At the command *march*, all the divisions, each conducted by its chief, will step off smartly, the guides standing fast; each odd division will wheel by file to the left around its right guide; each even division will wheel by file to the right around its left guide, each division

opposite guide, and when its head shall be up with this guide, the chief will halt the division, and cause it to face to the front.

357. Each division, on facing to the front, will be aligned by its chief by the right; to this end, the chiefs of the even divisions will move rapidly to the right of their respective divisions.

358. The divisions being aligned, each chief will command, FRONT; at this, the guides will shift to their proper flanks.

359. In a column with the left in front, the countermarch will be executed by the same commands and means; but all the divisions will be aligned by the left; to this end, the chiefs of the odd divisions will hasten to the left of their respective divisions as soon as the latter shall have been faced to the front.

360. The colonel, placed on the directing flank, will superintend the general movement.

361. The countermarch being ended, the lieutenant-colonel will always place himself abreast with the leading, and the major abreast with the rearmost division.

362. In a column by company, closed in mass, the countermarch will be executed by the same means and commands, applying to companies what is prescribed for divisions.

363. The countermarch will always take place from a halt, whether the column be closed in mass, or at full, or half distance.

ARTICLE XI.—*Being in column by company, closed in mass, to form divisions.*

 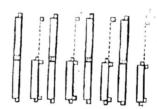

364. The column being closed in mass, right in front, and at a halt, when the colonel shall wish to form divisions, he will command:

1. *Form divisions.* 2. *Left companies, left*—FACE. 3. MARCH (or *double quick*—MARCH.)

365. At the first command, the captains of the left companies will caution them to face to the left.

366. At the second command, the left companies will face to the left, and their captains will place themselves by the side of their respective left guides.

367. The right companies, and their captains, will stand fast; but the right and left guides of each of these companies will place themselves respectively before the right and left files of the com-

SCHOOL OF THE BATTALION.

pany, both guides facing to the right, and each resting his right arm gently against the breast of the front rank man of the file, in order to mark the direction

368 At the command *march*, the left companies only will put themselves in march, their captains standing fast, as each shall see that his company, filing past, has nearly cleared the column, he will command

1. *Such company.* 2. HALT. 3. FRONT

369 The first command will be given when the company shall yet have four paces to march; the second at the instant it shall have cleared its right company and the third immediately after the second.

370. The company having faced to the front, the files, if there be intervals between them, will promptly incline to the right, the captain will place himself on the left of the right company of the division, and align himself correctly on the front rank of that company.

371 The left guide will place himself at the same time before one of the three left files of his company, face to the right, and cover correctly the guides of the right company, the moment his captain sees him established on the direction he will command

Right—DRESS

372 At this, the left company will dress forward on the alignment of the right company, the front rank man, who may find himself opposite the left guide, will, without preceding his rank, rest lightly his breast against the right arm of this guide, the captain of the left company will direct its alignment on this man, and the alignment being assured he will command. FRONT, but not quit his position

373 The colonel, seeing the divisions formed will command

Guides—POSTS

374 At this, the guides who have marked the fronts of divisions will return to their places in column, the left guide of each right company passing through the interval in the center of the division, and the captains will place themselves as prescribed, No 75

375 The colonel, from the directing flank of the column, will superintend the general execution of the movement

376. If the column be in march, instead of at a halt, when the colonel shall wish to form divisions, he will command

1. *Form divisions.* 2. *Left companies, by the left flank.* 3. MARCH
(or *double quick*—MARCH).

377 At the first command, the captains of the right companies will command, *Mark time*, the captains of the left companies will caution their companies to *face by the left flank*

378 At the third command the right companies will mark time, the left companies will ... the ... the captains of the

left companies will each see his company file past him, and when it has cleared the column, will command:

Such company by the right flank—MARCH.

As soon as the divisions are formed, the colonel will command:

4. *Forward.* 5. MARCH.

379. At the fifth command, the column will resume the gait at which it was marching previous to the commencement of the movement. The guides of each division will remain on the right and left of their respective companies; the left guide of the right company will pass into the line of file closers, before the two companies are united; the right guide of the left company will step into the rear rank. The captains will place themselves as prescribed, No. 75.

Being in column at full or half distance to form divisions.

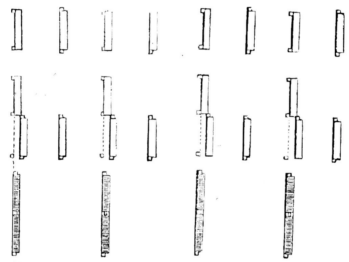

380. If the column be at a halt, and, instead of being closed in mass, is at full or half distance, divisions will be formed in the same manner; but the captains of the left companies, if the movement be made in quick time, after commanding FRONT, will each place himself before the center of his company, and command: 1. *Such company, forward.* 2. *Guide right.* 3. MARCH. If the movement be made in double quick time, each will command as soon as his company has cleared the column:

1. *Such company by the right flank.* 2. MARCH.

381. The right guide of each left company will so direct his march as to arrive by the side of the man on the left of the right company. The left company being nearly up with the rear rank

of the right company, its captain will halt it, and the movement will be finished as prescribed, No 371, and following.

382 If the left be in front, the movement will be executed by inverse means the right companies will conform themselves to what is prescribed above for the left companies and the two guides, placed respectively, before the right and left files of each left company, will face to the left. At the command, *Guides, posts*, given by the colonel, the guides, who have marked the front of divisions, and the captains, will quickly retake their places in the column.

383. If the column be marching at full distance, the divisions will be formed as prescribed, No. 196. If it be marching at half distance, the formation will take place by the commands and according to the principles indicated No. 376; if the column be marching in double quick time, the companies which should mark time will march in quick time by the command of their captains.

PART FOURTH.

ARTICLE II.—*Different modes of passing from column at full distance into line of battle*

1. To the left (or right)
2. On the right (or left)
3. Forward,
4. Faced to the rear,
} Into line of battle

1 *Column at full distance, right in front, to the left into line of battle.*

390. A column, right in front, being at a halt, when the colonel shall wish to form it to the left into line, he will assure the positions of the guides by the means previously indicated, and then command

1 *Left into line, wheel.* 2. MARCH (or *double quick*—MARCH).

391 At the first command, the right guide of the leading company will hasten to place himself on the direction of the left guides of the column, face to them, and place himself so as to be opposite to one of the three right files of his company, when they shall be in line he will be assured in this position by the lieutenant-colonel

392. At the command *march*, briskly repeated by the captains, the left front rank man of each company will face to the left, and rest his breast lightly against the right arm of his guide, the companies will wheel to the left on the principle of wheeling from a halt, conforming themselves to what is prescribed, school of the company, No 239· each captain will turn to his company, to observe the execution of the movement, and, when the right of the company shall arrive at three paces from the line of battle, he will command:

1. *Such company.* 2. HALT.

393 The company being halted, the captain will place himself

on the line by the side of the left front rank man of the company next on the right, align himself correctly, and command .

3 *Right*—DRESS.

394 At this command, the company will dress up between the captain and the front rank man on its left, the captain directing the alignment on that man, the front rank man on the right of the right company, who finds himself opposite to its right guide, will lightly rest his breast against the left arm of this guide

395. Each captain, having aligned his company, will command, FRONT, and the colonel will add

Guides—POSTS.

396 At this command, the guides will return to their places in line of battle, each passing through the nearest captain's interval, to permit him to pass, the captain will momentarily step before the first file of his company, and the covering sergeant behind the same file *This rule is general for all the formations into line of battle.*

397 When companies form line of battle, file closers will always place themselves exactly two paces from the rear rank, which will sufficiently assure their alignment,

398. The battalion being correctly aligned, the colonel, lieutenant-colonel, and major, as well as the adjutant and sergeant-major, will return to their respective places in line of battle *This rule is general for all the formations into line of battle,* nevertheless, the battalion being in the school of elementary instruction, the colonel will go to any point he may deem necessary

399 A column, with the left in front, will form itself *to the right into line of battle,* according to the same principles; the left guide of the left company will place himself, at the first command, on the direction of the right guides, in a manner corresponding to what is prescribed, No. 371, for the right guide of the right company.

400 At the command *guides, posts,* the captains will take their places in line of battle as well as the guides *This rule is general for all formations into line of battle in which the companies are aligned by the left*

401 A column by division may form itself into line of battle by the same commands, and means, but observing what follows if the right be in front, at the command *halt,* given by the chiefs of division, the left guide of each right company will place himself on the alignment opposite to one of the three files on the left of his company, the left guide of the first company will be assured on the direction by the lieutenant-colonel, the left guides of the other right companies will align themselves correctly on the division guides; to this end, the division guides (on the alignment) will invert, and hold their pieces up perpendicularly before the center of their bodies, at the command *left into line, wheel.* If the column by division be with the left in front, the right guides of

left companies will conform themselves to what has just been prescribed for the left guides of right companies, and place themselves on the line opposite to one of the three right files of their respective companies.

402. A column in march will be formed into line, without halting, by the same commands and means. At the command *march*, the guides will halt in their places, and the lieutenant-colonel will promptly rectify their positions.

403. If, in forming the column into line, the colonel should wish to move forward, without halting, he will command

1. *By companies, left wheel*   2. MARCH (or *double quick*—MARCH)

404. At the command *march*, briskly repeated by the captains, each company will wheel to the left on a fixed pivot, as prescribed in the school of the company, No. 261, the left guides will step back into the rank of file closers before the wheel is completed, and when the right of the companies shall arrive near the line, the colonel will command

3. *Forward*   4. MARCH   5. *Guide center.*

405. At the fourth command, given at the instant the wheel is completed, the companies will march directly to the front. At the fifth command, the color and the general guides will move rapidly six paces to the front. The colonel will assure the direction of the color, the captains of companies and the men will, at once, conform themselves to the principles of the march in line of battle, to be hereinafter indicated, No. 587, and following.

406. The same principles are applicable to a column left in front.

Column at full distance, on the right (or *on the left*), *into line of battle.*

414. A column by company, at full distance and right in front, having to form itself on the right into line of battle, the colonel will indicate to the lieutenant-colonel a little in advance, the point of *appui*, or rest, for the right, as well as the point of direction to the left; the lieutenant-colonel will hasten with two markers, and establish them in the following manner on the direction indicated.

415. The first marker will be placed at the point of *appui* for the right front rank man of the leading company; the second will indicate the point where one of the three left files of the same company will rest when in line; they will be placed so as to present the right shoulder to the battalion when formed.

416. These dispositions being made, the colonel will command:

1. *On the right, into line.*   2. *Battalion, guide right.*

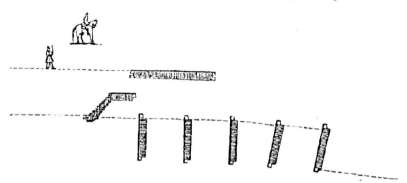

417. At the second command, the right will become the directing flank, and the touch of the elbow will be to that side; the right guide of the leading company will march straight forward until up with the turning point, and each following guide will march in the trace of the one immediately preceding.

418. The leading company being nearly up with the first marker, its captain will command: 1. *Right turn*, and when the company is precisely up with this marker, he will add: 2. MARCH.

419. At the command *march*, the company will turn to the right; the right guide will so direct himself as to bring the man next to him opposite to the right marker, and when at three paces from him, the captain will command:

1. *First company.*   2. HALT.

420. At the second command, the company will halt; the files, not yet in line, will form promptly; the left guide will retire as a file closer; and the captain will then command:

3. *Right!*—DRESS.

421. At this command, the company will align itself; the two men who find themselves opposite to the two markers, will each lightly rest his breast against the right arm of his marker; the captain, passing to the right of the front rank, will direct the alignment on these two men. *These rules are general for all successive formations.*

422. The second company will continue to march straight forward; when arrived opposite to the left flank of the preceding company, it will turn to the right, and be formed on the line of battle, as has just been prescribed; the right guide will direct himself so as to come upon that line by the side of the man on the left of the first company.

423. At the distance of three paces from the line of battle, the company will be halted by its captain, who will place himself briskly by the side of the man on the left of the preceding company, and align himself correctly on its front rank.

SCHOOL OF THE BATTALION.

424. The left guide will, at the same time, place himself before one of the three left files of his company, and, facing to the right, he will place himself accurately on the direction of the two markers of the preceding company

425. The captain will then command:

Right—DRESS.

426. At this command, the second company will dress forward on the line: the captain will direct its alignment on the front rank man who has rested his breast against the left guide of the company.

427. The following companies will thus come successively to form themselves on the line of battle, each conforming itself to what has just been prescribed for the one next to the right; and when they shall all be established, the colonel will command:

Guides—POSTS.

428. At this command, the guides will take their places in line of battle, and the markers placed before the right company will retire

429. If the column be marching in quick time, and the colonel should wish to cause the movement to be executed in double quick time, he will add the command: *Double quick*—MARCH. At the command *march*, all the companies will take the double quick step, and the movement will be executed as prescribed, No 417, and following.

430. The colonel will follow up the formation, passing along the front, and being always opposite to the company about to turn it is thus that he will be the better able to see and to correct the error that would result from a command given too soon or too late to the preceding company

431 The lieutenant-colonel will, with the greatest care, assure the direction of the guides; to this end, the instant that the markers are established for the leading company, he will move a little beyond the point at which the left of the next company will rest, establish himself correctly on the prolongation of the two markers, and assure the guide of the second company on this direction; this guide being assured, the lieutenant-colonel will place himself farther to the rear, in order to assure, in like manner, the guide of the third company, and so on successively, to the left of the battalion. In assuring the guides in their positions on the line of battle, he will take care to let them first place themselves, and confine himself to rectifying their positions if they do not cover accurately, and at the proper distance, the preceding guides or markers *This rule is general for all successive formations*

432 A column, left in front, will form itself on the left into line of battle according to the same principles, the captains will go to the left of their respective companies to align them, and shift afterwards to their proper flanks as prescribed No 400

134 SCHOOL OF THE BATTALION.

Column at full distance, forward into line of battle.

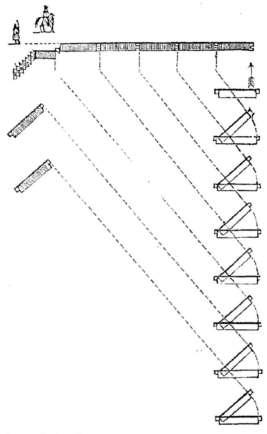

440. A column being by company, at full distance, right in front, and at a halt, when the colonel shall wish to form it forward into line, he will conform to what is prescribed Nos. 414 and 415, and then command:

1. *Forward into line.* 2. *By company, left half wheel.* 3. MARCH (or *double quick*—MARCH).

441. At the first command, the captain of the leading company will add—*guide right*, put the company in march, halt it three paces from the markers, and align it against the latter by the right.

442. At the command *march*, all the other companies will wheel to the left on fixed pivots; and, at the instant the colonel shall judge, according to the direction of the line of battle, that the companies have sufficiently wheeled, he will command:

4. *Forward.* 5. MARCH. 6. *Guide right.*

443. At the fifth command, the companies, ceasing to wheel, will

march straight forward, and at the sixth, the men will touch elbows toward the right. The right guide of the second company, who is nearest to the line of battle, will march straight forward, each succeeding right guide will follow the file immediately before him at the cessation of the wheel.

444. The second company having arrived opposite to the left file of the first, its captain will cause it to turn to the right, in order to approach the line of battle, and when its right guide shall be at three paces from that line, the captain will command

1. *Second company.* 2. HALT.

455. At the second command, the company will halt; the files not yet in line with the guide will come into it promptly, the left guide will place himself on the line of battle, so as to be opposite to one of the three files on the left of the company, and, as soon as he is assured on the direction by the lieutenant-colonel, the captain, having placed himself accurately on the line of battle, will command

3. *Right*—DRESS.

446. At the instant that the guide of the second company begins to turn to the right, the guide of the third, ceasing to follow the file immediately before him, will march straight forward, and, when he shall arrive opposite to the left of the second, his captain will cause the company to turn to the right, in order to approach the line of battle, halt it at three paces from that line, and align it by the right, as prescribed for the second company.

447. Each following company will execute what has just been prescribed for the third, as the preceding company shall turn to the right, in order to approach the line of battle.

448. The formation ended, the colonel will command

Guides—POSTS.

449. The colonel and lieutenant-colonel will observe, in this formation, what is prescribed for them on the right into line.

450. A column left in front, will form itself forward into line of battle, according to the same principles, and by inverse means.

451. When a column by company at full distance, right in front, and in march shall arrive behind the right of the line on which it is to form into battle, the colonel and lieutenant-colonel will conform themselves to what is prescribed Nos. 414 and 415.

452. The head of the column having arrived at company distance from the two markers established on the line, the colonel will command:

1. *Forward into line.* 2. *By company, left half wheel.* 3. MARCH
(or *double quick*—MARCH.)

453. At the first command, the captain of the first company will command, *Guide right*, and caution it to march directly to the front, th   ·   ·   ·   them to wheel t   ·

454 At the command *march*, briskly repeated by the captains, the first company will continue to march to the front, taking the touch of elbows to the right Its chief will halt it at three paces from the markers, and align it by the right. The other companies will wheel to the left on fixed pivots, and at the instant the colonel shall judge that they have wheeled sufficiently, he will command ·

4. *Forward.* 5. MARCH. 6. *Guide right.*

455. At the fifth command, the companies will cease to wheel and move forward At the sixth, they will take the touch of elbows to the right. The movement will be executed as previously explained.

456. If the colonel should wish to form the column forward into line, and to continue to march in this order, he will not cause markers to be established; the movement will be executed in *double quick time*, by the same commands and means, but with the following modifications

457 At the first command, the captain of the first company will add *quick time* after the command *guide right* At the second command, the first company will continue to march in quick time, and will take the touch of elbows to the right, its chief will immediately place himself on its right, and to assure the march, will take points of direction to the front. The captain of the second company will cause his company to take the same gait as soon as it shall arrive on a line with the first, and will also move to the right of his company; the captains of the third and fourth companies will execute successively what has just been prescribed for the second The companies will preserve the touch of elbows to the right, until the command, *guide center.*

458. When the color company shall have entered the line, the colonel will command, *guide center.* At this command, the color-bearer and the right general guide will move rapidly six paces in advance of the line. The colonel will assure the direction of the color-bearer The lieutenant-colonel and the right companies will immediately conform themselves to the principles of the march in line of battle The left companies and the left general guide, as they arrive on the line, will also conform to the same principles. If the column be marching in double quick time, when the last company shall have arrived on the line, the colonel will cause the double quick to be resumed

459 It is not necessary that the movement be entirely completed, before halting the battalion. As soon as the part of the battalion already formed shall have arrived on the line of battle, the colonel will halt the battalion; the companies not in line will each complete the movement.

SCHOOL OF THE BATTALION. 137

Column at full distance, faced to the rear, into line of battle.

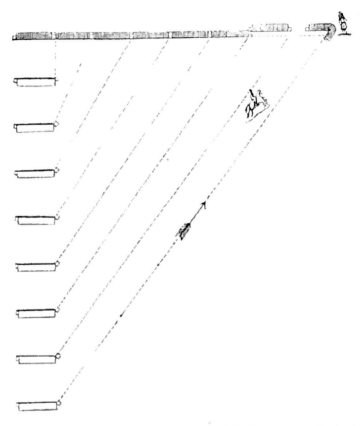

466. A column being by company, at full distance, right in front, and at a halt, when the colonel shall wish to form it into line faced to the rear, he and the lieutenant-colonel will conform themselves to what is prescribed Nos. 414 and 415, and the colonel will then command:

1. *Into line, faced to the rear.* 2. *Battalion, right*—FACE. 3. MARCH (or *double quick*—MARCH).

467. At the first command, the captain of the leading company will cause it to face to the right, and put it in march, causing it to wheel by file to the left, and direct its march towards the line of battle which it will pass in rear of the left marker; the first file having passed three paces beyond the line, the company will wheel again by file to the left, in order to place itself in rear of the two **markers**; being in this position, its captain will halt it, face it to the front

468. At

to the right, each captain placing himself by the side of his right guide

469. At the command *march*, the companies will put themselves in movement, the left guide of the second, who is nearest to the line of battle, will hasten in advance to mark that line, he will place himself on it as prescribed above for successive formations, and thus indicate to his captain the point at which he ought to pass the line of battle, by three paces, in order to wheel by file to the left, and then to direct his company parallelly to that line

470. As soon as the first file of this company shall have arrived near the left file of the preceding one already on the line of battle, its captain will command

1. *Second company.* 2. Halt. 3. Front. 4. *Right*—Dress.

471. The first command will be given when the company shall yet have four paces to take to reach the halting point

472. At the second command, the company will halt

473. At the third, the company will face to the front, and if there be openings between the files, the latter will promptly close to the right; the captain will immediately place himself by the side of the man on the left of the preceding company, and align himself on its front rank

474. The fourth command will be executed as prescribed, No. 426

475. The following companies will be conducted and established on the line of battle as just prescribed for the second, each regulating itself by the one that precedes it, the left guides will detach themselves in time to precede their respective companies on the line by twelve or fifteen paces, and each place himself so as to be opposite to one of the three left files of his company, when in line If the movement be executed in double quick time, the moment it is commenced, all the left guides will detach themselves at the same time from the column, and will move at a run, to establish themselves on the line of battle

476. The formation ended, the colonel will command

Guides—Posts.

477. The colonel and lieutenant-colonel, in this formation, will each observe what is prescribed for him in that of *on the right, into line of battle*

478. A column, left in front, will form itself faced to the rear into line of battle according to the same principles and by inverse means.

479. If the column be in march, and should arrive in front of the right of the line on which it is to form into battle, the colonel and lieutenant-colonel will conform to what is prescribed, Nos 414 and 415.

480. When the head of the column shall be nearly at company distance from the two markers established on the line, the colonel will command·

1 *Into line, faced to the rear.* 2 *Battalion, by the right flank.* 3 MARCH (or *double quick*—MARCH.)

481. At the first command, the captains will caution their companies to face by the right flank.

482. At the command *march,* briskly repeated by the captains of companies, all the companies will face to the right, the first company will then wheel by file to the left, and be directed by its captain a little to the rear of the left marker, then pass three paces beyond the line, and wheel again by file to the left, having arrived on the line, the captain will halt the company, and align it by the right. The remaining part of the movement will be executed as heretofore explained.

483. The foregoing principles are applicable to a column, left in front.

484. As the companies approach the line of battle, it is necessary that their captains should so direct the march as to cross that line a little in rear of their respective guides, who are faced to the basis of the formation; hence each guide ought to detach himself in time to find himself correctly established on the direction before his company shall come up with him.

ARTICLE III.—*Formation in line of battle by two movements.*

485. If a column by company, right in front and at a halt, find itself in part on the line of battle, and the colonel should think proper to form line of battle before all the companies enter the new direction, the formation will be executed in the following manner.

486. It will be supposed that the column has arrived behind the line of battle, and that five companies have entered the new direction. The colonel having assured the guides of the first five companies on the direction, will command:

1. *Left into line, wheel.* 2. *Three rear companies, forward into line.*

487. At the second command, the chief of each of the rear companies will command: *By company, left half wheel,* and the colonel will add:

3. MARCH (or *double quick*—MARCH.)

488. At this command, briskly repeated, the first five companies will form themselves *to the left, into line of battle,* and the three last *forward, into line of battle,* by the means prescribed for these respective formations; each captain of the three rear companies will, when his company shall have sufficiently wheeled, command:

1. *Forward.* 2. MARCH. 3. *Guide right.*

489. If the column be in march, the colonel will command:

1. *To the left, and forward into line.* 2. MARCH (or *double quick*—MARCH.)

490.

company, left half wheel. At the command *march*, briskly repeated, the first five companies will form left into line, and the last three forward into line, as prescribed for these respective formations. Those captains who form their companies forward into line will conform to what is prescribed, No. 488.

491. If the colonel should wish, in forming the battalion into line, to march it immediately forward, he will command:

1. *By company to the left, and forward into line.* 2. MARCH.

492. At the first command, each captain, whose company is not yet in the new direction, will command: 1. *By company, left half wheel;* 2. *Double quick.* At the command *march*, briskly repeated by the captains, the companies not in the new direction will execute what is prescribed above for forming forward into line while marching; each of the other companies will wheel to the left on a fixed pivot, and when the right of these companies shall arrive on the line, the colonel will command:

3. *Forward.* 4. MARCH. 5. *Guide center.*

493. The fifth command will be given when the color-bearer arrives on the line, if not already there.

494. If the battalion be marching in double quick time, the colonel will cause quick time to be taken before commencing the movement.

495. If, instead of arriving behind, the column should arrive before the line of battle, the colonel will command:

1. *Left into line, wheel.* 2. *Three rear companies into line, faced to the rear.*

496. At the second command, the captain of each of the three rear companies will command: 1. *Such company;* 2. *Right*—FACE. The colonel will then add:

3. MARCH (or *double quick*—MARCH.)

497. At this command, briskly repeated, the first five companies will form themselves *to the left, into line of battle,* and the three last *faced to the rear, into line of battle,* by the means prescribed for these respective formations.

498. If the column be in march, the colonel will command:

1. *To the left, and into line faced to the rear.* 2. MARCH (or *double quick*—MARCH.)

499. The movement will be executed as prescribed Nos. 391, 480, and following.

500. These several movements in a column, left in front, will be executed according to the same principles, and by inverse means

ARTICLE IV.—*Different modes of passing from column at half distance, into line of battle.*

1. To the left (or right)
2. On the right (or left)
3. Forward, by deployment,
4. Faced to the rear,
} into line of battle

1st *Column at half distance, to the left (or right) into line of battle.*

501 A column at half distance having to form itself to the left (or right) into line of battle, the colonel will cause it to take distances by one of the means prescribed, Article IX, Part Third, of this school, which being executed, he will form the column into line of battle, as has been indicated, No 390, and following

502 If a column by company, at half distance, be in march, and it be necessary to form rapidly into line of battle, the colonel will command

1 *By the rear of column left (or right) into line, wheel* 2. MARCH (*or double quick*—MARCH)

503. At the first command, the right general guide will move rapidly to the front, and place himself a little beyond the point where the head of the column will rest, and on the prolongation of the guides The captain of the eighth company will command. *Left into line, wheel,* the other captains will caution their companies to continue to march to the front.

504 At the command *march*, briskly repeated by the captain of the eighth company, the guide of this company will halt short, and the company will wheel to the left, conforming to the principles prescribed for wheeling from a halt; when its right shall arrive near the line, the captain will halt the company and align it by the left The other captains will place themselves briskly on the flank of the column, when the captain of the seventh sees there is sufficient distance between his company and the eighth to form the latter into line, he will command. *Left into line, wheel*—MARCH; the left guide will halt short, and facing to the rear, will place himself on the line, the company will wheel to the left, the man on the left of the front rank will face to the left, and place his breast against the left arm of the guide, the captain will halt the company when its right shall arrive near the line, and will align it by the left The other companies will conform successively to what has just been prescribed for the seventh.

505 Each captain will direct the alignment of his company on the left man in the front rank of the company next on his right.

506 The lieutenant-colonel will be watchful that the leading guide marches accurately on the prolongation of the line of battle, and directs himself on the right general guide. The major, placed in the rear of the left guide of the eighth company, will, as soon as the guide of the seventh company is established on the direction, hasten in rear of the guides of the other companies, so as to assure each of them in succession on the li-

2d Column at half distance, on the right (or left) into line of battle.

507 A column at half distance will form itself on the right (or left) into line of battle, as prescribed for a column at full distance

3d Column at half distance, forward, into line of battle

508. If it be wished to form a column at half distance, forward into line of battle, the colonel will first cause it to close in mass and then deploy it on the leading company

4th Column at half distance, faced to the rear, into line of battle.

509 A column at half distance will be formed into line of battle, faced to the rear, as prescribed for a column at full distance

ARTICLE V —*Deployment of columns closed in mass*

510. A column in mass may be formed into line of battle:
1 Faced to the front by the deployment
2 Faced to the rear, by the countermarch and the deployment
3. Faced to the right and faced to the left by a change of direction by the flank, and the deployment

511 When a column in mass, by division, arrives behind the line on which it is intended to deploy it, the colonel will indicate, in advance, to the lieutenant-colonel, the direction of the line of battle as well as the point on which he may wish to direct the column. The lieutenant-colonel will immediately detach himself, with two markers, and establish them on that line, the first at the point indicated, the second a little less than the front of a division from the first

512 Deployments will always be made upon lines parallel, and lines perpendicular to the line of battle, consequently, if the head of the column be near the line of battle, the colonel will commence by establishing the direction of the column perpendicularly to that line, if it be not already so, by one of the means indicated, No. 211 and following, or No. 307 and following If the column be in march, he will so direct it that it may arrive exactly behind the markers, perpendicularly to the line of battle, and halt it at three paces from that line

513. The column, right in front, being halted, it is supposed that the colonel wishes to deploy it on the first division; he will order the left general guide to go to a point on the line of battle a little beyond that at which the left of the battalion will rest when deployed, and place himself correctly on the prolongation of the markers established before the first division

514 These dispositions being made, the colonel will command·

1. *On the first direction, deploy column.* 2 *Battalion left*—FACE.

515 At the first command, the chief of the first division will cause it to stand fast. the chiefs of the three other divisions will remind them that they will have to face to the left

516 At the second command, the three last divisions will face to the left, the chief of each division will place himself by the side

SCHOOL OF THE BATTALION.

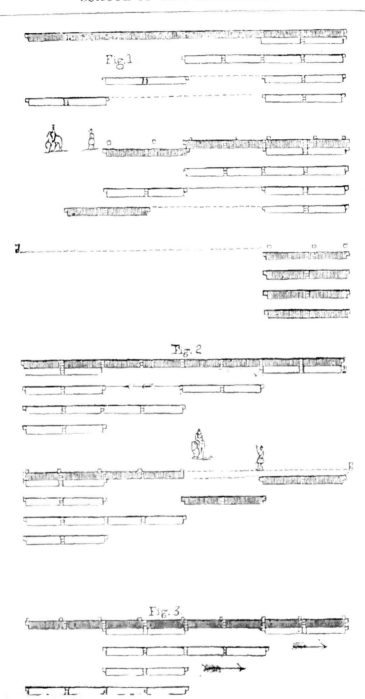

Fig. 1

Fig. 2

Fig. 3

of its left guide, and the junior captain by the side of the covering sergeant of the left company, who will have stepped into the front rank.

517. At the same command, the lieutenant-colonel will place a third marker on the alignment of the two first, opposite to one of the three left files of the right company, first division, and then place himself on the line of battle a few paces beyond the point at which the left of the second division will rest.

518. The colonel will then command:

3. MARCH (or *double quick*—MARCH.)

519. At this command, the chief of the first division will go to its right, and command:

Right—DRESS.

520. At this, the division will dress up against the markers; the chief of the division, and its junior captain, will each align the company on his left, and then command:

FRONT.

521. The three divisions, faced to the left, will put themselves in march; the left guide of the second will direct himself parallelly to the line of battle; the left guides of the third and fourth divisions will march abreast with the guide of the second; the guides of the third and fourth, each preserving the prescribed distance between himself and the guide of the division which preceded his own in the column.

522. The chief of the second division will not follow its movement; he will see it file by him, and when its right guide shall be abreast with him, he will command:

1. *Second division.* 2. HALT. 3. FRONT.

523. The first command will be given when the division shall yet have seven or eight paces to march; the second, when the right guide shall be abreast with the chief of the division, and the third immediately after the second.

524. At the second command, the division will halt; at the third, it will face to the front, and if there be openings between the files, the chief of the division will cause them to be promptly closed to the right; the left guides of both companies will step upon the line of battle, face to the right, and place themselves on the direction of the markers established before the first division, each guide opposite to one of the three left files of his company.

525. The division having faced to the front, its chief will place himself accurately on the line of battle, on the left of the first division; and when he shall see the guides assured on the direction, he will command, *Right*—DRESS. At this, the division will be aligned by the right in the manner indicated in the first.

526. The third and fourth divisions will continue to march: at the command *halt*, given to the second, the chief of the third will halt

in his own person, place himself exactly opposite to the guide of the second, after this division shall have faced to the front and closed its files; he will see his division file past, and when his right guide shall be abreast with him, he will command:

1. *Third division.* 2. Halt. 3. Front.

527. As soon as the division faces to the front, its chief will place himself two paces before its center, and command:

1. *Third division, forward.* 2. *Guide right.* 3. March.

528. At the third command, the division will march toward the line of battle; the right guide will so direct himself as to arrive by the side of the man on the left of the second division, and when the division is at three paces from the line of battle, its chief will halt it and align it by the right.

529. The chief of the fourth division will conform himself (and the chief of the fifth, if there be a fifth) to what has just been prescribed for the third.

530. The deployment ended, the colonel will command:

Guides—Posts.

531. At this command, the guides will resume their places in line of battle, and the markers will retire.

532. If the column be in march, and the colonel shall wish to deploy it on the first division without halting the column, he will make the dispositions indicated Nos. 512 and 513, and when the first division shall arrive at three paces from the line, he will command:

1. *On the first division, deploy column.* 2. *Battalion by the left flank.* 3. March (or *double quick*—March).

533. At the first command, the chief of the first division will caution it to halt, and will command, *First division;* the other chiefs will caution their divisions to face by the left flank.

534. At the command *march*, briskly repeated by the chiefs of the rear divisions, the chief of the first divison will command, Halt, and will align his division by the right against the markers; the other divisions will face to the left, their chiefs hastening to the left of their divisions. The second division will conform its movements to what is prescribed Nos. 522, and following. The third and fourth divisions will execute what is prescribed Nos. 526, and following; but the chief of each division will halt in his own person at the command march, given by the chief of the division which precedes him, and when the right of his division arrives abreast of him, he will command:

Such division, by the right flank—March.

535. The lieutenant-colonel will assure the position of the guides, conforming to what is prescribed No. 431. The major will follow the movement abreast with the fourth division.

536. If the colonel shall wish to deploy the column without halting it, and to continue the march, the markers will not be posted; the movement will be executed by the same commands and the same means as the foregoing, but with the following modifications:

537. At the first command, the chief of the first division will command, 1. *Guide right.* 2. *Quick time.* At the command, *Double quick*—MARCH, given by the colonel, the first division will march in quick time and will take the touch of elbows to the right; the captains will place themselves on the right of their respective companies; the captain on the right of the battalion will take points on the ground to assure the direction of the march. The chief of the second division will allow his division to file past him, and when he sees its right abreast of him, he will command, 1. *Second division, by the right flank.* 2. MARCH. 3. *Guide right,* and when this division shall arrive on the alignment of the first, he will cause it to march in quick time. The third and fourth divisions will deploy according to the same principles as the second.

538. The colonel, lieutenant-colonel, major and color-bearer will conform themselves to what is prescribed No. 458.

539. The colonel will see, pending the movement, that the principles just prescribed are duly observed, and particularly that the divisions, in deploying, be not halted too soon nor too late. He will correct promptly and quickly the faults that may be committed, and prevent their propagation. *This rule is general for all deployments.*

540. The column being at a halt, if, instead of deploying it on the first, the colonel shall wish to deploy it on the rearmost division, he will cause the dispositions to made indicated No. 511, and following; but it will be the right general guide whom he will send to place himself beyond the point at which the right of the battalion will rest when deployed.

541. The colonel will then command:

1. *On the fourth* (or such) *division, deploy column.* 2, *Battalion, right* —FACE.

542. At the first command, the chief of the fourth division will caution it to stand fast; the chiefs of the other divisions will caution them that they will have to face to the right.

543. At the second command, the first three divisions will face to the right; and the chief of each will place himself by the side of its right guide.

544. At the same command, the lieutenant-colonel will place a third marker between the first two, so that this marker may be opposite to one of the three right files of the left company of the division; the lieutenant-colonel will then place himself on the line of battle a few paces beyond the point at which the right of the third division will rest when deployed.

545. The colonel will then command:

3. MARCH (or *double quick*—MARCH).

546. At this command, the three right divisions will put themselves in march, the guide of the first so directing himself as to pass three paces within the line marked by the right general guide. The chief of the third division will not follow its movement; he will see it file past, halt it when its left guide shall be abreast with him, and cause it to face to the front; and, if there be openings between the files, he will cause them to be promptly closed to the left.

547. The chief of the fourth division, when he sees it nearly unmasked by the three others will command:

1. *Fourth division, forward.* 2. *Guide left.* 3. MARCH.

548. At the command *march*, which will be given the instant the fourth is unmasked, this division will approach the line of battle, and when at three paces from the markers on that line, its chief will halt it, and command:

Left—DRESS.

549. At this command, the division will dress forward against the markers; the chief of the division and the junior captain will each align the company on his right, and then command:

FRONT.

550. The instant that the third division is unmasked, its chief will cause it to approach the line of battle, and halt it in the manner just prescribed for the fourth.

551. The moment the division halts, its right guide and the covering sergeant of its left company will step on the line of battle, placing themselves on the prolongation of the markers established in front of the fourth division; as soon as they shall be assured in their positions, the division will be aligned as has just been prescribed for the fourth.

552. The second and first divisions which will have continued to march, will, in succession, be halted and aligned by the left, in the same manner as the third; the chiefs of these divisions will conform themselves to what is prescribed, No. 526. The second being near the line of battle, the command will not be given for it to move on this line but it will be dressed up to it.

553. The deployment ended, the colonel will command:

Guides—POSTS.

554. At this command, the chiefs of division and the guides will resume their places in line of battle, and the markers will retire.

555. The lieutenant-colonel will assure the positions of the guides by the means indicated, No. 431, and the major will follow the movement abreast with the fourth division.

556. If the column be in march, and the colonel shall wish to deploy it on the fourth division, he will make the dispositions indicated, No. 511 and following; and when the head of the column shall arrive within three paces of the line, he will command:

1. *On the fourth division, deploy column.* 2. *Battalion, by the right flank.* 3. MARCH (or *double quick*—MARCH).

557. At the first command, the chief of the fourth division will caution it to halt, and will command, *Fourth division;* the chiefs of the other divisions will caution their divisions to face to the right.

558. At the command *march*, briskly repeated by the chiefs of the first three divisions, the chief of the fourth will command: HALT. The first three divisions will face to the right, and be directed parallelly to the line of battle. The chief of each of these divisions will place himself by the side of its right guide. The chief of the third division will see his division file past him, and when his left guide is abreast of him, he will halt it, and face it to the front. The chief of the fourth division, when he shall see it nearly unmasked, will command: 1. *Fourth division, forward;* 2. *Guide left;* 3. MARCH (or *double quick*—MARCH). The division will move towards the line of battle, and when at three paces from this line, it will be halted by its chief, and aligned by the left.

559. The chief of the third division will move his division forward, conforming to what has just been prescribed for the fourth.

560. The chiefs of the second and first divisions, after halting their divisions, will conform to what is prescribed, No. 552.

561. If the colonel should wish to deploy on the fourth division without halting the column, and to continue to march forward, he will not have markers posted, and the movement will be executed by the same commands and the same means, with the following modifications: the fourth division, when unmasked, will be moved forward in quick time, and will continue to march, instead of being halted, and will take the touch of elbows to the left. The third division, on being unmasked, will be moved to the front in double quick time, but when it arrives on the alignment of the fourth it will take the quick step, and dress to the left until the command *Guide center,* is given by the colonel. The chiefs of the second and first divisions will conform to what has been prescribed for the third. When the first division shall arrive on the line, the colonel may cause the battalion to take the double quick step.

562. The colonel and lieutenant-colonel will conform to what has been prescribed, Nos. 458 and 459.

563. To deploy the column on an interior division, the colonel will cause the line to be traced by the means above indicated, and the general guides will move briskly on the line, as prescribed, Nos. 513 and 540. This being executed, the colonel will command: 1. *On such division, deploy column.* 2. *Battalion outwards*—FACE. 3. MARCH (or *double quick*—MARCH).

564. Whether the column be with the right or left in front, the divisions which, in the order in battle, belong to the right of the directing one, will face to the right; the others, except the directing division, will face to the left; the divisions in front of the latter will deploy by the means indicated, No. 542, and following; those in its rear will deploy as is prescribed, No. 513, and following.

SCHOOL OF THE BATTALION.

565. The directing division, the instant it finds itself unmasked, will approach the line of battle, taking the guide left or right, according as the right or left of the column may be in front. The chief of this division will align it by the directing flank, and then step back into the rear, in order momentarily to give place to the chief of the next for aligning the next division.

566. The lieutenant-colonel will assure the positions of the guides of divisions, which, in the line of battle, take the right of the directing division, and the major will assure the positions of the other guides.

567. If the column be in march, the colonel will command:

1. *On such division, deploy column.* 2. *Battalion, by the right and left flanks.* 3. MARCH (or *double quick*—MARCH).

568. The divisions which are in front of the directing one will deploy by the means indicated, Nos. 557, and following; those in rear, as prescribed, No. 533, and following.

569. The directing division, when unmasked, will conform to what is prescribed for the fourth division, No. 558.

570. The colonel, lieutenant-colonel and major will conform to what has been prescribed, Nos. 458 and 459.

571. In a column, left in front, deployments will be executed according to the same principles, and by inverse means.

PART FIFTH.

ARTICLE II —*Oblique march in line of battle.*

623. The battalion marching in line of battle, when the colonel shall wish to cause it to oblique, he will command

1. *Right* (or *left*) *oblique.* 2. MARCH (or *double quick*—MARCH).

624. At the first command, the major will place himself in front of, and faced to the color-bearer.

625. At the command *march*, the whole battalion will take the oblique step. The companies and captains will strictly observe the principles established in the School of the Company.

626. The major in front of the color-bearer ought to maintain the latter in a line with the center corporal, so that the color-bearer may oblique neither more nor less than that corporal. He will carefully observe also that they follow parallel directions and preserve the same length of step.

627. The lieutenant-colonel will take care that the captains and the three corporals in the center keep exactly on a line and follow parallel directions.

628. The colonel will see that the battalion preserves its parallelism; he will exert himself to prevent the files from opening or crowding. If he perceive the latter fault, he will cause the files on the flank, to which the battalion obliques, to open out.

629. The colonel wishing the direct march to be resumed, will command·

1. *Forward.* 2. MARCH.

630. At the command *march*, the battalion will resume the direct march. The major will place himself thirty paces in front of the color-bearer, and face to the colonel, who will establish him, by a signal of the sword, on the direction which the color-bearer ought to pursue. The latter will immediately take two points on the ground between himself and the major.

631. In resuming the direct march, care will be taken that the men do not close the intervals which may exist between the files at once; it should be done almost insensibly.

ARTICLE III.—*To halt the battalion, marching in line of battle, and to align it.*

635. The battalion, marching in the line of battle, when the colonel shall wish to halt it, he will command:

1. *Battalion.* 2. HALT.

636. At the second command, the battalion will halt; the color-rank and the general guides will remain in front; but if the colonel should not wish immediately to resume the advance in line, nor to give a general alignment, he will command:

Color and general guides—POSTS.

637. At this command, the color-rank and general guides will retake their places in line of battle, the captains in the left wing will shift to the right of their companies.

638. If the colonel should then judge it necessary to rectify the alignment, he will command:

Captains, rectify the alignment.

639. The captains will immediately cast an eye towards the center, align themselves accurately, on the basis of the alignment, which the lieutenant-colonel will see well directed, and then promptly dress their respective companies. The lieutenant-colonel will admonish such captains as may not be accurately on the alignment by the command: *Captain of* (such) *company,* or *captains of* (such) *companies, move up or fall back.*

640. But when the colonel shall wish to give the battalion a general alignment, either parallel or oblique, instead of rectifying it as above, he will move some paces outside of one of the general guides (the right will here be supposed) and caution the right general guide and the color-bearer to face him, and then establish them by signal of the sword, on the direction which he may wish to give to the battalion. As soon as they shall be correctly established, the left general guide will place himself on their direction, and be assured in his position by the major. The color-bearer will carry the color-lance perpendicularly between his eyes, and the two corporals of his rank will return to their places in the front rank the moment he shall face to the colonel.

641. This disposition being made, the colonel will command:

1. *Guides*—ON THE LINE.

SCHOOL OF THE BATTALION. 151

642. At this command, the right guide of each company in the right wing, and the left guide of each company in the left, will each place himself on the direction of the color-bearer, and the two general guides, face to the color-bearer, place himself in rear of the guide who is next before him, at a distance equal to the front of his company, and align himself upon the color-bearer and the general guide beyond.

643. The captains in the right wing will shift to the left of their companies, except the captain of the color-company, who will remain on its right, but step into the rear rank; the captains in the left wing will shift to the right of their companies.

644. The lieutenant colonel will promptly rectify, if necessary, the positions of the guides of the right wing, and the major those of the other; which being executed, the colonel will command:

2. *On the center*—DRESS.

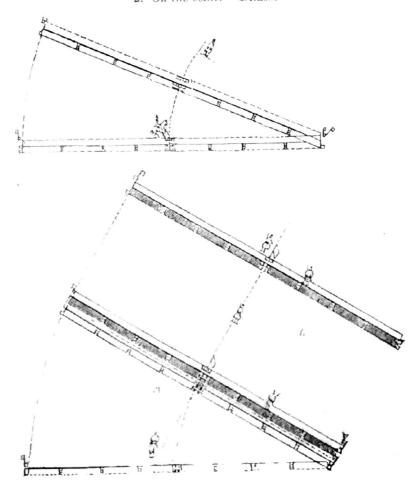

645. At this command, the companies will move up in quick time against the guides, where, having arrived, each captain will align his company according to prescribed principles, the lieutenant colonel aligning the color-company

646. If the alignment be oblique, the captains will take care to conform their companies to it in conducting them towards the line.

647 The battalion being aligned, the colonel will command·

3. *Color and guides*—Posts.

648. At this command, the color-bearer, the general and company guides, and the captains in the right wing, will take their places in the line of battle, and the color-bearer will replace the heel of the color-lance against his right hip.

649. If the new direction of the line of battle be such that one or more companies find themselves in advance of that line, the colonel, before establishing the general guides on the line, will cause such companies to be moved to the rear, either by the back step, or by first facing about, according as there may be less or more ground to be repassed to bring the companies in rear of the new direction.

650 When the colonel shall wish to give a general alignment, and the color and general guides are not on the line, he will cause them to move out by the command:

1. *Color and general guides*—On the Line

651 At this command, the color-bearer and the general guides will place themselves on the line, conforming to what is prescribed, No. 640.

Article IV.—*Change of direction in marching in line of battle.*

652. The battalion marching in line of battle, when the colonel shall wish it to change direction to the right, he will command:

1. *Change direction to the right* 2. March (or *double quick—* March)

653. At the command *march*, the movement will commence; the color-rank will shorten the step to fourteen or seventeen inches, and direct itself circularly to the right, taking care to advance the left shoulder, but only insensibly; the major will place himself before the color-bearer, facing him, and so direct his march that he may describe an arc of a circle neither too large nor too small; he will also see that the color-bearer takes steps of fourteen or seventeen inches, according to the gait

654 The right general guide will wheel on the right captain of the battalion as his pivot, the left general guide will circularly march in the step of twenty-eight inches or thirty-three inches, according to the gait, and will align himself upon the color-bearer and the right general guide

655. The corporal placed in the center of the battalion, will take steps of fourteen or seventeen inches, and will wheel to the

right by advancing insensibly the left shoulder; the battalion will conform itself to the movement of the center; to this end, the captain of the color-company, and the captain of the next to the left, will attentively regulate their march, as well as the direction of their shoulders, on the three center corporals. All the other captains will regulate the direction of their shoulders and the length of their step on this basis.

656. The men will redouble their attention in order not to pass the line of captains.

657. In the left wing, the pace will be lengthened in proportion as the file is distant from the center; the captain of the eighth company who closes the left flank of the battalion will take steps of twenty-eight or thirty-three inches, according to the gait.

658. In the right wing the pace will be shortened in proportion as the file is distant from the center; the captain who closes the right flank will only slowly turn in his person, observing to yield ground a little if pushed.

659. The colonel will take care to prevent the center of the battalion from describing an arc of a circle, either too great or too small, in order that the wings may conform themselves to its movement. He will see also that the captains keep their companies constantly aligned upon the center, so that there may be no opening and no crowding of files. He will endeavor to prevent faults, and, should they occur, correct them without noise.

660. The lieutenant-colonel, placed before the battalion, will give his attention to the same objects.

661. When the colonel shall wish the direct march to be resumed, he will command:

1. *Forward.* 2. MARCH.

662. At the command *march*, the color-rank, the general guides, and the battalion will resume the direct march; the major will immediately place himself thirty or forty paces in front, face to the colonel, placed in rear of the center, who will establish him by signal of the sword on the perpendicular direction which the corporal in the center of the battalion ought to pursue; the major will immediately cause the color-bearer, if necessary, to incline to the right or left, so as to be exactly opposite to his file; the color-bearer will then take two points on the ground between himself and the major.

663. The lieutenant-colonel will endeavor to give to the color-company and the next on the left a direction perpendicular to that pursued by the center corporal, and all the other companies, without precipitancy, will conform themselves to that basis.

ARTICLE V.—*To march in retreat, in line of battle.*

664. The battalion being halted, if it be the wish of the colonel to cause it to march in retreat, he will command:

1. *Face to the rear.* 2. *Battalion about.* FACE.

665. At the second command, the battalion will face about; the color-rank and the general guides, if in advance, will take their places in line; the color-bearer will pass into the rear rank, now leading; the corporal of his file will step behind the corporal next on his own right, to let the color-bearer pass, and then step into the front rank, now rear, to re-form the color-file; the colonel will place himself behind the front rank, become the rear; the lieutenant-colonel and major will place themselves before the rear rank, now leading.

666. The colonel will take post forty paces behind the color file, in order to assure the lieutenant-colonel on the perpendicular, who will place himself at a like distance in front, as prescribed for the advance in line of battle.

667. If the battalion be the one charged with the direction, the colonel will establish markers in the manner indicated, No. 589, except that they will face to the battalion, and that the first will be placed twenty-five paces from the lieutenant-colonel. If the markers be already established, the officer charged with replacing them in succession will cause them to face about, the moment that the battalion executes this movement, and then the marker nearest to the battalion will hasten to the rear of the two others.

668. These dispositions being made, the colonel will command:

3. *Battalion, forward.*

669. At this command, the color-bearer will advance six paces beyond the rank of file closers, accompanied by the two corporals of his guard of that rank, the center corporal stepping back to let the color-bearer pass; the two file closers nearest this center corporal will unite on him behind the color-guard to serve as a basis of alignment for the line of file closers; the two general guides will place themselves abreast with the color rank, the covering sergeants will place themselves in the line of file closers, and the captains in the rear rank, now leading; the captains in the left wing, now right, will, if not already there, shift to the left of their companies, now become the right.

670. The colonel will then command:

4. MARCH (or *double quick*—MARCH.)

671. The battalion will march in retreat on the same principles which govern the advance in line: the center corporal behind the color-bearer will march exactly in his trace.

672. If it be the directing battalion, the color-bearer will direct himself on the markers, who will, of their own accord, each place himself in succession behind the marker most distant, on being approached by the battalion; the officer charged with the superintendence of the markers will carefully assure them on the direction.

673. In the case of a subordinate battalion, the color-bearer will maintain himself on the perpendicular by means of points taken on the ground.

674. The colonel, lieutenant-colonel and major will each discharge the same functions as in the advance in line.

675. The lieutenant-colonel, placed on the outside of the file closers of the color company, will also maintain the three file closers of the basis of alignment in a square with the line of direction: the other file closers will keep themselves aligned on this basis

ARTICLE VI — *To halt the battalion marching in retreat, and to face it to the front.*

676. The colonel having halted the battalion, and wishing to face it to the front, will command:

1. *Face to the front.* 2. *Battalion, about*—FACE.

677. At the second command, the color-rank, general guides, captains and covering sergeants, will all retake their habitual places in line of battle, and the color-bearer will repass into the front rank.

678. The battalion marching in line of battle by the front rank, when the colonel shall wish to march it in retreat, he will command:

1. *Battalion, right about.* 2. MARCH.

679. At the command *march*, the battalion will face to the rear and move off at the same gait by the rear rank. The principles prescribed Nos. 669 and following will be carefully observed.

680. If the colonel should wish the battalion to march again by the front, he will give the same commands.

ARTICLE VII — *Change of direction, in marching in retreat.*

681. A battalion retiring in line will change direction by the commands and means indicated No. 652 and following; the three file closers, united behind the color rank, will conform themselves to the movement of this rank, and wheel like it; the center file closer of the three will take steps of fourteen or seventeen inches, according to the gait, and keep himself steadily at the same distance from the color-bearer; the line of file closers will conform themselves to the movement of its center, and the lieutenant-colonel will maintain it on that basis.

ARTICLE VIII.—*Passage of obstacles, advancing and retreating.*

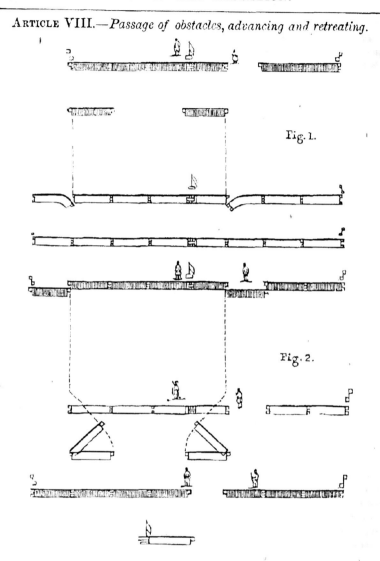

682. The battalion advancing in line will be supposed to encounter an obstacle which covers one or more companies; the colonel will cause them to ploy into column at full distance, in rear of the next company towards the color, which will be executed in the following manner. It will be supposed that the obstacle only covers the third company, the colonel will command:

Third company, obstacle.

683. At this command, the captain of the third company will place himself in its front, turn to it, and command, 1. *Third com-*

pany, *by the left flank, to the rear into column.* 2. *Double quick.* 3. MARCH. He will then hasten to the left of his company.

684. At the command *march*, the company will face to the left in marching; the two left files will promptly disengage to the rear in double quick time; the left guide placing himself at the head of the front rank, will conduct it behind the fourth company, directing himself parallelly with this company; the captain of the third will himself halt opposite to the captain of the fourth, and see his company file past; when its right file shall be nearly up with him, he will command, 1. *Third company.* 2. *By the right flank.* 3. MARCH. 4. *Guide right*, and place himself before the center of his company.

685. At the command *march*, the company will face to the right, preserving the same gait, but the moment it shall be at the prescribed distance, its captain will command:

1. *Quick time.* 2. MARCH.

686. This company will thus follow in column that behind which it finds itself, and at wheeling distance, its right guide marching exactly in the trace of the captain of that company.

687. As soon as the third company shall have faced to the left, the left guide of the second will place himself on the left of the front rank of his company, and maintain between himself and the right of the fourth the space necessary for the return into line of the third.

688. The obstacle being passed, the colonel will command:

Third company, forward into line.

689. At this command, the captain turning to his company, will add:

1. *By company, right half wheel.* 2. *Double quick.* 3. MARCH.

690. At the command *march*, the company will take the double quick step, and execute a half wheel; its captain will then command, 1. *Forward.* 2. MARCH. 3. *Guide left.* The second command will be given when the company shall have sufficiently wheeled.

691. At the command *march*, the company will direct itself straight forward toward the line of battle, and retake its position in it according to the principles prescribed for the formation forward into line of battle.

692. It will be supposed that the obstacle covers several contiguous companies (the three companies on the right for example), the colonel will command:

158 SCHOOL OF THE BATTALION.

1. *Three right companies, obstacle.* 2. *By the left flank, to the rear, into column.* 3. *Double quick*—MARCH.

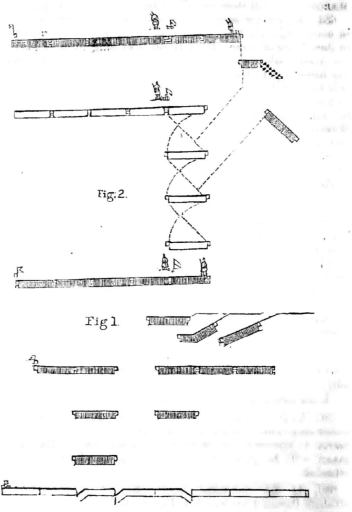

693. At the first command, the captains of the designated companies will each place himself before the center of his company, and caution it as to the movement about to be executed.

694. At the command *march*, the designated companies will face to the left in marching, and immediately take the double quick step; each captain will cause the head of his company to disengage itself to the rear, and the left guide will place himself at the head of the front rank; the captain of the third company will conform himself to what is prescribed No. 684, and following; the captains of the other companies will conduct them by the flank

in rear of the third, inclining toward the head of the column; and as the head of each company arrives opposite to the right of the one next before it in column, its captain will himself halt, see his company file past, and conform himself for facing it to the front, in marching, to what is prescribed No. 684, and following.

695. When the last company in column shall have passed the obstacle, the colonel will command:

1. *Three right companies, forward, into line.*

696. At this command, the captain of each of these three companies will command, *By company, right half wheel.* The colonel will then add:

1. *Double quick.* 2. MARCH.

697. At this, briskly repeated by the captains of the three companies, each company will conform itself to what is prescribed No. 690, and following.

698. It is supposed, in the foregoing examples, that the companies belonged to the right wing; if they make part of the other, they will execute the passage of an obstacle according to the same principles and by inverse means.

699. When flank companies are broken off to pass an obstacle, the general guide on that flank will place himself six paces in front of the outer file of the nearest company to him remaining in line.

700. In the preceding movements, it has been supposed that the battalion was marching in quick time, but if it be marching in double quick time, and the colonel shall wish to cause several contiguous companies to break to _____ will first order the bat-

709. When a battalion, retiring in line, shall encounter a defile which it must pass, the colonel will halt the battalion, and face it to the front.

710. It will be supposed that the defile is in rear of the left flank, and that its width is sufficient to give passage to a column by platoon; the colonel will place a marker fifteen or twenty paces in rear of the file closers at the point around which the subdivisions will have to change direction in order to enter the defile; he will then command:

To the rear, by the right flank, pass the defile.

711. The captain of the first company will immediately command:

will afterwards successively put themselves into line by the oblique step, as the ground may permit.

705. If the battalion be marching in retreat in double quick time, and many contiguous companies be marching before the rear rank of the battalion, the colonel will not change the gait of the battalion in causing them to re-enter into line.

706. When the color-company shall be obliged to execute the movement of passing an obstacle, the color-bearer will return into line at the moment the company shall face to the left or right; the major will place himself six paces before the extremity of the company behind which the color-company marches in column, in order to give the step and the direction; he, himself, first taking the step from the battalion.

707. As soon as the color-company shall have returned into line, the front rank of the color-guard will again move out six paces in front of the battalion, and take the step from the major; the latter will immediately place himself twenty or thirty paces in front of the color-bearer, and face to the colonel placed behind the center of the battalion, who will establish him on the perpendicular; and as soon as he shall be assured on it, the color-bearer will instantly take two points on the ground between himself and the major.

708. It is prescribed, as a general rule, that the companies of the right wing ought to execute the movement of passing obstacles by the left flank, and the reverse for companies of the other wing; but if the obstacle cover at once several companies of the center, each will file into column behind that, still in line, and of the same wing, which may be th

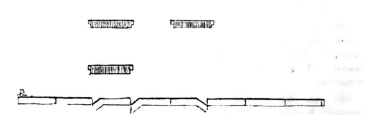

693. At the first command, the captains of the designated companies will each place himself before the center of his company, and caution it as to the movement about to be executed.

694. At the command *march*, the designated companies will face to the left in marching, and immediately take the double quick step; each captain will cause the head of his company to disengage itself to the rear, and the left guide will place himself at the head of the front rank; the captain of the third company will conform himself to what is prescribed No. 684, and following; the captains of the other companies will conduct them by the flank

SCHOOL OF THE BATTALION. 161

ARTICLE IX.—*To pass a defile, in retreat, by the right or left flank.*

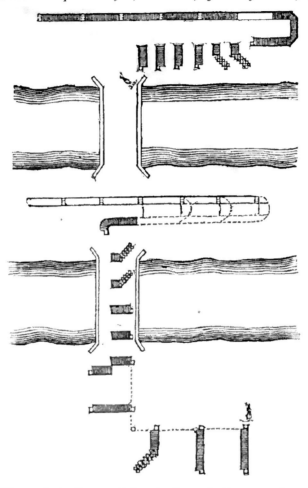

709. When a battalion, retiring in line, shall encounter a defile which it must pass, the colonel will halt the battalion, and face it to the front.

710. It will be supposed that the defile is in rear of the left flank, and that its width is sufficient to give passage to a column by platoon; the colonel will place a marker fifteen or twenty paces in rear of the file closers at the point around which the subdivisions will have to change direction in order to enter the defile; he will then command:

To the rear, by the right flank, pass the defile.

711. The captain of the first company will immediately command:

1. *First company, right*—FACE. 2. MARCH (or *double quick—* MARCH).

712. At the command *march*, the first company will commence the movement; the first file will wheel to the right, march to the rear till it shall have passed four paces beyond the file closers, when it will wheel again to the right, and then direct itself straight forward toward the left flank. All the other files of this company will come to wheel in succession at the same place where the first had wheeled.

713. The second company will execute, in its turn, the same movement, by the commands of its captain, who will give the command MARCH, so that the first file of his company may immediately follow the last of the first, without constraint, however, as to taking the step of the first; the first file of the second company will wheel to the right, on its ground; all the other files of this company will come in succession to wheel at the same place. The following companies will execute, each in its turn, what has just been prescribed for the second.

714. When the whole of the second company shall be on the same direction with the first, the captain of the first will cause it to form, by platoon, into line, and the moment that it is in column the guide of the first platoon will direct himself on the marker around whom he has to change direction in order to enter the defile.

715. The second company will continue to march by the flank, direcing itself parallelly with the line of battle; and it, in its turn, will form, by platoon, into line, when the third company shall be wholly on the same direction with itself.

716. The following companies will successively execute what has just been prescribed for the second, and each will form, by platoon, into line, when the next company shall be on the same direction with itself.

717. The first platoon of the leading company, having arrived opposite to the marker placed at the entrance of the defile, will turn to the left, and the following platoons will all execute this movement at the same point. As the last companies will not be able to form platoons before reaching the defile, they will so direct themselves, in entering it, as to leave room to the left for this movement.

718. The battalion will thus pass the defile by platoon; and, as the two platoons of each company shall clear it, companies will be successively formed by the means indicated, School of the Company, No. 273, and following.

719. The head of the column having cleared the defile, and having reached the distance at which the colonel wishes to re-form line faced to the defile, he may cause the leading company to turn to the left, to prolong the column in that direction, and then form it to the left into line of battle; or he may halt the column, and form it into line of battle, faced to the rear.

720. If the defile be in the rear of the right flank, it will be passed by the left; the movement will be executed according to the same principles, and by inverse means.

721. If the defile be too narrow to receive the front of a platoon, it will be passed by the flank. Captains and file closers will be watchful that the files do not lose their distances in marching. Companies or platoons will be formed into line as the width of the defile may permit, or as the companies shall successively clear it.

ARTICLE X.—*To march by the flank.*

722. The colonel, wishing the battalion to march by the flank, will command:

1. *Battalion.* 2. *Right* (or *left*)—FACE. 3. *Forward.* 4. MARCH (or *double quick* —MARCH).

723. At the second command, the captains and covering sergeants will place themselves as prescribed. Nos. 136 and 141, School of the Company.

724. The sergeant on the left of the battalion will place himself to the left and by the side of the last file of his company, covering the captains in file.

725. The battalion having to face by the left flank, the captains, at the second command, will shift rapidly to the left of their companies, and each place himself by the side of the covering sergeant of the company preceding his own, except the captain of the left company, who will place himself by the side of the sergeant on the left of the battalion. The covering sergeant of the right company will place himself by the right side of the front rank man of the rearmost file of his company, covering the captains in file.

726. At the command *march*, the battalion will step off with life; the sergeant, placed before the leading file (right or left in front), will be careful to preserve exactly the length and cadence of the step, and to direct himself straight forward; to this end he will take points on the ground.

727. Whether the battalion march by the right or left flank, the lieutenant-colonel will place himself abreast with the leading file, and the r⋯ ⋯file l⋯ ⋯of the front ran⋯

728. The adjutant, placed between the lieutenant-colonel and the front rank, will march in the same step with the head of the battalion, and the sergeant-major, placed between the major and the color-bearer, will march in the same step with the adjutant

729 The captains and file closers will carefully see that the files neither open out, nor close too much, and that they regain insensibly their distances, if lost

730. The colonel wishing the battalion to wheel by file, will command

   1. *By file right* (or *left*). 2 MARCH.

731 The files will wheel in succession, and all at the place where the first had wheeled, in conforming to the principles prescribed in the School of the Company.

732. The battalion marching by the flank, when the colonel shall wish it to halt, he will command

   1 *Battalion*. 2 HALT. 3 FRONT.

733 These commands will be executed as prescribed in the School of the Company, No. 146

734 If the battalion be marching by the flank, and the colonel should wish to cause it to march in line, either to the front or to the rear, the movements will be executed by the commands and means prescribed in the School of the Company.

ARTICLE XI — *To form the battalion on the right or left, by file, into line of battle.*

735 The battalion marching by the right flank, when the colonel shall wish to form it on the right by file, he will determine the line of battle, and the lieutenant-colonel will place two markers on that line, in conformity with what is prescribed, No. 415

736 The head of the battalion being nearly up with the first marker, the colonel will command:

   1. *On the right, by file, into line.* 2 MARCH (or *double quick—* MARCH).

737 At the command *march*, the leading company will form itself on the right by file, into line of battle, as indicated in the School of the Company, No. 149; the front rank man of the first file will rest his breast lightly against the right arm of the first marker, the other companies will follow the movement of the leading company, each captain will place himself on the line at the same time with the front rank man of his first file, and on the right of this man.

738 The left guide of each company, except the leading one, will place himself on the direction of the markers, and opposite to the left file of his company, at the instant that the front rank man of this file arrives on the line

739. The formation being ended, the colonel will command:

   Guides—POSTS.

SCHOOL OF THE BATTALION. 165

740. The colonel will superintend the successive formation of the battalion, moving along the front of the line of battle.

741. The lieutenant-colonel will, in succession, assure the direction of the guides, and see that the men of the front rank, in placing themselves on the line, do not pass it.

742. If the battalion march by the left flank, the movement will be executed according to the same principles, and by inverse means.

Article XII.—*Changes of front.*

Change of front perpendicularly forward.

743. The battalion being in line of battle, it is supposed to be the wish of the colonel to cause a change of front forward on the right company, and that the angle formed by the old and new positions be a right angle, or a few degrees more or less than one; he will cause two markers to be placed on the new direction, before the position to be occupied by that company, and order its captain to establish it against the markers.

744. The captain of the right company will immediately direct it upon the markers by a wheel to the right on the fixed pivot; and after having halted it, he will align it by the right.

745. These dispositions being made, the colonel will command:

1. *Change front forward on first company.* 2. *By company, right half wheel.* 3. March (or *double quick*—March).

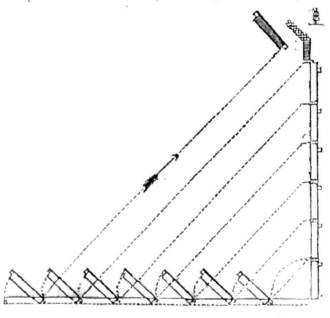

746. At the second command, each captain will place himself before the centre of his company.

747. At the third, each company will wheel to the right on the fixed pivot, the left guide of each will place himself on its left as soon as he shall be able to pass, and when the colonel shall judge that the companies have sufficiently wheeled, he will command:

4. *Forward.* 5. MARCH. 6. *Guide right.*

748. At the fifth command, the companies ceasing to wheel will march straight forward, at the sixth, the men will touch elbows towards the right.

749. The right guide of the second company will march straight forward until this company shall arrive at the point where it should turn to the right, each succeeding right guide will follow the file immediately before him at the cessation of the wheel, and will march in the trace of this file until this company shall turn to the right to move upon the line, this guide will then march straight forward.

750. The second company having arrived opposite to the left file of the first, its captain will cause it to turn to the right, the right guide will direct himself so as to arrive squarely upon the line of battle, and when he shall be at three paces from that line, the captain will command:

1. *Second company.* 2. HALT.

751. At the second command, the company will halt, the files not yet in line with the guide will come into it promptly, the left guide will place himself on the line of battle, and as soon as he is assured in the direction by the lieutenant-colonel, the captain will align the company by the right.

752. Each following company will conform to what has just been prescribed for the second.

753. The formation ended, the colonel will command

Guides—POSTS.

754. If the battalion be in march, and the colonel shall wish to change front forward on the first company, and that the angle formed by the old and new positions be a right angle, he will cause two markers to be placed on the new direction, before the position to be occupied by that company, and will command:

1. *Change front forward on first company.* 2. *By company, right half wheel.* 3. MARCH (or *double quick*—MARCH).

755. At the first command, the captains will move rapidly before the center of their respective companies, the captain of the first company will command: 1. *Right turn;* 2. *Quick time;* the captains of the other companies will caution them to wheel to the right.

756. At the command *march*, the first company will turn to the right according to the principles prescribed in the school of the soldier, No 402; its captain will halt it at three paces from the markers, and the files in rear will promptly come into line. The captain will align the company by the right.

757. Each of the other companies will wheel to the right on a fixed pivot; the left guides will place themselves on the left of their respective companies, and when the colonel shall judge they have wheeled sufficiently, he will command:

4. *Forward.* 5. MARCH. 6. *Guide right.*

758. These commands will be executed as indicated No. 746 and following.

759. The colonel will cause the battalion to change front forward on the eighth company according to the same principles and by inverse means.

Change of front perpendicularly to the rear.

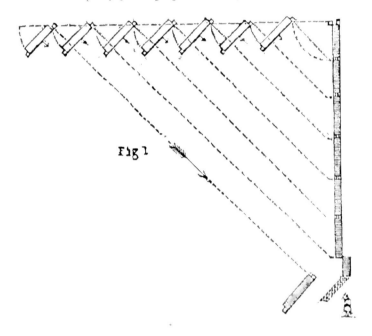

168 SCHOOL OF THE BATTALION.

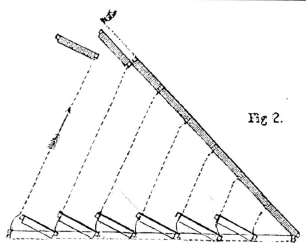

Fig 2.

760. The colonel, wishing to change front to the rear on the right company, will impart his purpose to the captain of this company. The latter will immediately face his company about, wheel it to the left on the fixed pivot, and halt it when it shall be in the direction indicated to him by the colonel; the captain will then face his company to the front, and align it by the right against the two markers, whom the colonel will cause to be established before the right and left files.

761. These dispositions being made, the colonel will command:

1. *Change front to the rear, on first company.* 2. *Battalion, about—*FACE. 3. *By company, left half wheel.* 4. MARCH (or *double quick—*MARCH).

762. At the second command, all the companies, except the right, will face about.

763. At the third, the captains, whose companies have faced about, will each place himself behind the center of his company, two paces from the front rank, now the rear.

764. At the fourth, these companies will wheel to the left on the fixed pivot by the rear rank; the left guide of each will, as soon as he is able to pass, place himself on the left of the rear rank of his company, now become the right; and when the colonel shall judge that the companies have sufficiently wheeled, he will command:

5. *Forward.* 6. MARCH. 7. *Guide left.*

765. At the sixth command, the companies will cease to wheel, march straight forward towards the new line of battle, and, at the seventh, take the touch of the elbow towards the left.

766. The guide of each company on its right flank, become left, will conform himself to the principles prescribed, No. 748.

767. The second company, from the right, having arrived opposite to the left of the first, will turn to the left; the guide will so

direct himself as to arrive parallelly with the line of battle, cross that line, and when the front rank, now in the rear, shall be three paces beyond it, the captain will command: 1. *Second company.* 2. HALT.

768. At the second command, the company will halt; the files which may not yet be in line with the guide, will promptly come into it; the captain will cause the company to face about, and then align it by the right.

769. All the other companies will execute what has just been prescribed for the second, each as it successively arrives opposite to the left of the company that precedes it on the new line of battle.

770. The formation being ended, the colonel will command:

Guides—POSTS.

771. The colonel will cause a change of front on the left company of the battalion to the rear, according to the same principles and by inverse means.

772. In changes of front, the colonel will give a general superintendence to the movement.

773. The lieutenant-colonel will assure the direction of the guides as they successively move out on the line of battle, conforming himself to what has been prescribed in the successive formations.

ARTICLE XIII.—*To ploy the battalion into column doubled on the center.*

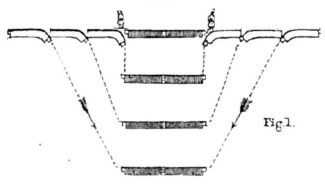

Fig. 1.

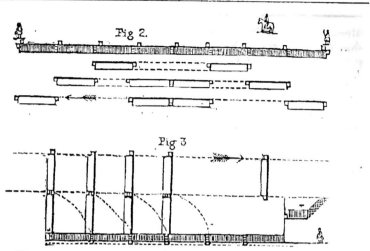

776. This movement consists in ploying the corresponding companies of the right and left wings into column at company distance, or closed in mass, in rear of the two center companies, according to the principles prescribed, Article III., Part II., of this School.

777. The colonel, wishing to form the double column at company distance, (the battalion being in line of battle,) will command:

1. *Double column, at half distance.* 2. *Battalion, inwards*—FACE. 3. MARCH (or *double quick*—MARCH).

778. At the first command, the captains will place themselves two paces in front of their respective companies; the captains of the two center companies will caution them to stand fast, and the other captains will caution their companies to face to the left and right, respectively. The covering sergeants will step into the front rank.

779. At the second command, the fourth and fifth companies will stand fast; the others of the right wing will face to the left, and the others of the left wing will face to the right; each captain whose company has faced, will hasten to break to the rear the two files at the head of his company; the left guide of each right company, and the right guide of each left company, will each place himself at the head of its front rank, and the captain by the side of his guide.

780. At the command *march*, the fourth and fifth companies, which are to form the first division, will stand fast; the senior captain of the two will place himself before the center of the division and command: *Guide right;* the junior captain will place himself in the interval between the two companies, and the left guide of the left company will place himself in the front rank on the left of the division, as soon as he shall be able to pass.

781. All the other companies, conducted by their captains, will

SCHOOL OF THE BATTALION. 171

step off with life to arrange themselves in column at company distance, each company behind the preceding one in the column of the same wing, so that, in the right wing, the third may be next behind the fourth, the second next to the third, and so on to the right company, and, in the left wing, the sixth may be next behind the fifth, the seventh next to the sixth, and so on to the left company of the battalion

782. The corresponding companies of the two wings will unite into divisions in arranging themselves in column, an instant before the union, at the center of the column, the left guides of right companies will pass into the line of file closers, and each captain will command 1. *Such company;* 2 *Halt,* 3. FRONT

783 At the second command, which will be given at the instant of union, each company will halt; at the third, it will face to the front The senior captain in each division will place himself on its right, and command, *Right*—DRESS, and the junior captain will place himself in the interval between the two companies The division being aligned, its chief will command FRONT, and take his position two paces before its center

784. The column being thus formed, the divisions will take the respective denominations of *first, second, third, &c*, according to position in the column, beginning at the front

785. The lieutenant-colonel, who, at the second command, given by the colonel, will have placed himself at a little more than company distance in rear of the right guide of the first division, will assure the right guides on the direction as they successively arrive, by placing himself in their rear

786 The music will pass to the rear of the column

787 The battalion being in march, to form the double column at company distance without halting the battalion, the colonel will command·

1. *Double column at half distance.* 2. *Battalion by the right and left flanks.* 3 MARCH (or *double quick*—MARCH)

788 At the first command, each captain will move briskly in front of the center of his company, the captains of the fourth and fifth will caution their companies to march straight forward, the other captains will caution their companies to face to the right and left.

789 At the command *march*, the fourth and fifth companies will continue to march straight forward, the senior captain will place himself before the center of his division, and command· *Guide right;* the junior captain will place himself in the interval between the two companies The left guide of the fifth company will place himself on the left of the front rank of the division. The men will take the touch of elbows to the right The color and general guides will retake their places The three right companies will face to the left, and the three left companies will face to the right. Each captain will break to the rear two files at the head of his company the left guide of the right companies & the right

guides of the left companies, will each place himself at the head of the front rank of his company, and the captain by the side of his guide.

790. The third and sixth companies will enter the column and direct themselves parallelly to the first division. Each of the other companies will, in like manner, place itself behind the company of the wing to which it belongs, and will be careful to gain as much ground as possible toward the head of the column.

791. The corresponding companies of each wing will unite into divisions on taking their positions in column, and each captain, the instant the head of his company arrives at the center of the column, will command 1. *Such company, by the right (or left) flank.* 2. MARCH The senior captain of the two companies will place himself in front of the center of his division, and command *Guide right;* the junior captain will place himself in the interval between the two companies. The two companies, thus formed into a division, will take the touch of elbows to the right, and when each division has gained its proper distance, its chief will cause it to march in quick time.

792. When the battalion presents an odd number of companies, the formation will be made in like manner, and the company on either flank which shall find itself without a corresponding one, will place itself at company distance behind the wing to which it belongs.

793. The double column, closed in mass, will be formed according to the same principles, and by the same commands, substituting the indication, *closed in mass,* for that of *at half distance.*

794. The double column never being formed when two or more battalions are to be in one general column, it will habitually take the guide to the right, sometimes to the left, or in the center of the column, in the last case, the command will be, *guide center.* The column will march and change direction according to the principles prescribed for a simple column by division.

795. The double column at company distance will be closed in mass, or, if in mass, will take half distance, by the commands and means indicated for a simple column by division.

Deployment of the double column, faced to the front.

796. The colonel, wishing to deploy the double column, will place a marker respectively before the right and left files of the first division, and a third before the left file of the right company, same division, which being done, he will cause the two general guides to spring out on the alignment of the markers a little beyond the points at which the respective flanks of the battalion ought to rest, he will then command

1. *Deploy column.* 2. *Battalion outwards*—FACE. 3. MARCH (or double quick—MARCH).

797. The column will deploy itself on the two companies at its head, according to the principles prescribed for the deployment of

SCHOOL OF THE BATTALION. 173

column in mass. The captains of these companies will each, at the command *march*, place himself on the right of his own company, and align it by the right; the captain of the fourth will then place himself in the rear rank, and the covering sergeant in the rank of file closers, at the moment the captain of the third shall come to its left to align it.

798. The deployment being ended, the colonel will command:

Guides—POSTS.

799. If it be the wish of the colonel to cause the fire to commence pending the deployment, he will give an order to that effect to the captains of the fourth and fifth companies, and the fire will be executed according to the principles prescribed No. 438.

800. The battalion being in double column and in march, if the colonel shall wish to deploy it without halting the column, he will cause three markers to be posted on the line of battle, and when the head of the column shall arrive near the markers he will command

1. *Deploy column.* 2. *Battalion, by the right and left flanks.* 3. MARCH (or *double quick*—MARCH).

801. The column will deploy on the two leading companies, according to the principles prescribed for the deployment of a close column No. 533, and following, at the command *march*, the chief of the first division will halt it, and the captains of the fourth and fifth companies will align their companies by the right.

802. If the column be in march, and it be the wish of the colonel to deploy the column and to continue to march in the order of battle, he will not cause markers to be established at the head of the column. The movement will be executed by the commands and means indicated No. 800, observing what follows. At the first command, the chief of the first division will command, *Quick time.* At the command *march*, the first division will continue to march in quick time, the colonel will command, *Guide center.* The captains of the fourth and fifth companies, the color and the men, will immediately conform to the principles of the march in line of battle. The companies will take the quick step by the command of their captains as they successively arrive in line. The movement completed, the colonel may cause the battalion to march in double quick time.

To form the double column into line of battle, faced to the right or left.

803. The double column, being at company distance and at a halt, may be formed into line of battle faced to the right or left; when the colonel shall wish to form it faced to the right, he will command

1. *Right into line wheel, left companies on the right into line.* 2. *Battalion, guide right.* 3. MARCH (or *double quick*—MARCH.)

804. At the first command, each captain will place himself before th⋯ ⋯ ⋯ ⋯ be cau-

tioned that they will have to wheel to the right into line, the left companies that they will have to march straight forward.

805. At the second command, the left guide of the fourth company will place himself briskly on the direction of the right guides of the column, face to them, and opposite to one of the three last files of his company when in line of battle the lieutenant-colonel will assure him in that position.

806. At the command *march*, briskly repeated by all the captains, the right companies will form *to* the right into line of battle, the left companies will put themselves in march in order to form *on* the right into line of battle, these formations will be executed by the means indicated No 391 and following, and No 416 and following, the lieutenant-colonel will assure the guides of the left wing on the line of battle as they successively come upon it

807 If the column be in march, the colonel will command

1 *Right into line wheel* 2 *Left companies, on the right into line.* 3. *Battalion, guide right* 4 MARCH (or *double quick*—MARCH)

808 At the first command, each captain will place himself promptly before the center of his company; the right companies will be cautioned that they will have to wheel to the right, and the left companies that they will have to form on the right into line

809. At the command *march*, briskly repeated, the right companies will form to the right into line, and the left companies on the right into line These formations will be executed as prescribed Nos. 402, 417, and following

810. If the colonel should wish to move the battalion forward, at the moment the right companies have completed the wheel, he will command·

5. *Forward.* 6 MARCH (or *double quick*—MARCH)

811. At the command *forward*, the captains of the right companies will command, *Quick time* At the command *march*, the right companies will cease to wheel and march straight forward The colonel will then add·

7. *Guide center.*

812. The movement of the left companies will be executed in double quick time as prescribed above, and as they arrive on the line each captain will cause his company to march in quick time

813. The column may be formed faced to the left into line of battle according to the same principles

814. If the column be closed in mass instead of at company distance, these movements will be executed according to the principles prescribed Nos. 417, 502 and 510.

ARTICLE XIV.—*Dispositions against Cavalry.*

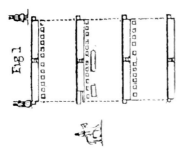
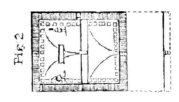

817. A battalion being in column by company, at full distance, right in front, and at a halt, when the colonel shall wish to form it into square, he will first cause divisions to be formed; which being done, he will command:

1. *To form square.* 2. *To half distance, close column.* 3. March (or *double quick*—March.)

818. At the command *march*, the column will close to company distance, the second division taking its distance from the rear rank of the first division.

819. At the moment of halting the fourth division, the file closers of each company of which it is composed, passing by the outer flank of their companies, will place themselves two paces before the front rank opposite to their respective places in line of battle, and face towards the head of the column.

820. At the commencement of the movement, the major will place himself on the right of the column abreast with the first division; the buglers formed in two ranks will place themselves at platoon distance, behind the inner platoons of the second division.

821. These dispositions being made, the colonel may, according to circumstances, put the column in march, or cause it to form square; if he wish to do the latter, he will command:

1. *Form square.* 2. *Right and left into line, wheel.*

822. At the first command, the lieutenant-colonel, facing to the left guides, and the major, facing to those of the right, will align them, from the front, on the respective guides of the fourth division, who will stand fast, holding up their pieces, inverted perpendicularly; the right guides, in placing themselves on the direction, will take their exact distances.

823. At the second command, the chief of the first division will caution it to stand fast; all the captains of the second and third divisions will place themselves before the centers of their respective companies and caution them that they will have to wheel, the right companies to the right, and the left companies to the left into line of battle.

824. T' closers, opposite by the

corporal of his file, who is in the rear rank, the corporal of the same file who is in the rank of file closers will step into the rear rank.

825. The chief of the fourth division will command: 1. *Fourth division forward,* 2. *Guide left,* and place himself at the same time two paces outside of its left flank.

826. These dispositions ended, the colonel will command:

MARCH (or *double quick*—MARCH)

827. At this command, briskly repeated, the first division will stand fast, but its right file will face to the right, and its left file to the left.

828. The companies of the second and third divisions will wheel to the right and left into line, and the buglers will advance a space equal to the front of a company.

829. The fourth division will close up to form the square, and when it shall have closed, its chief will halt it, face it about, and align it by the rear rank upon the guides of the division, who will for this purpose, remain faced to the front. The junior captain will pass into the rear rank, now become the front, and the covering sergeant of the left company will place himself behind him in the front rank, become rear. The file closers will at the same time close up a pace on the front rank, and the outer file on each flank of the division will face outwards

830 The square being formed, the colonel will command

Guides—POSTS.

831. At this command, the chiefs of the first and fourth divisions, as well as the guides, will enter the square

832 The captains whose companies have formed to the right into line, will remain on the left of their companies; the left guide of each of those companies will, in the rear rank, cover his captain, and the covering sergeant of each will place himself as a file closer behind the right file of his company

833. The field and staff will enter the square, the lieutenant-colonel placing himself behind the left, and the major behind the right of the first division.

834 If the battalion present ten, instead of eight companies, the fourth division will make the same movements prescribed above for the second and third divisions, and the fifth, the movements prescribed for the fourth division.

835. A battalion ought never to present, near the enemy's cavalry, an odd company. The odd company, under that circumstance, ought, when the battalion is under arms, to be consolidated, for the time, with the other companies.

836. The fronts of the square will be designated as follows. the first division will always be the *first front*; the last division, the *fourth front,* the right companies of the other divisions will form the *second front;* and the left companies of the same divisions the *third front.*

SCHOOL OF THE BATTALION. 177

837. A battalion being in column by company, at full distance, right in front, and in march, when the colonel shall wish to form square, he will cause this movement to be executed by the commands and means indicated, No. 817.

838. At the command *march*, the column will close to company distance, as is prescribed, No. 278. When the chief of the fourth division shall command *Quick march*, the file closers of this division will place themselves before the front rank.

839. The major and the buglers will conform to what is prescribed, No. 820.

840. If the colonel shall wish to form square, he will command:

1. *Form square.* 2. *Right and left into line, wheel.* 3. MARCH.

841. At the first command, the chief of the first division will caution it to halt, all the captains of the second and third divisions will rapidly place themselves before the centers of their respective companies, and caution them that they will have to wheel, the right companies to the right, and the left companies to the left into line. The chief of the fourth division will caution it to continue its march, and will hasten to its left flank. At the third command briskly repeated, the chief of the first division will halt his division and align it to the left, the outer files will face to the right and left, the rest of the movement will be executed as prescribed No. 828 and following.

842. The lieutenant-colonel and the major, at the command *march*, will conform to what is prescribed, No. 822.

843. If the battalion, before the square is formed, be in double column, the two leading companies will form the first front, the two rear companies the fourth; the other companies of the right half battalion will form the second, and those of the left half battalion the third front.

844. The first and fourth fronts will be commanded by the chiefs of the first and fourth divisions, each of the other two by its senior captain.

845. The commander of each front will place himself four paces behind its present rear rank, and will be replaced momentarily in the command of his company by the next in rank therein.

846. If the column be at full distance, instead of at company distance, as has been supposed, the square will be formed in the manner prescribed, No. 817 or 838, and following; and the dispositions indicated, Nos. 819 and 820, will be executed at the command *form square.*

847. If the column by division, whether double or simple, be in mass, and the colonel shall wish to form it into square, he will first cause it to take company distance; to this effect, he will command:

1. *To form square.* 2. *By the head of column, take half distance.*

848. The divisions will take half distance by the means indicated, No. 324, and following. What is prescribed, No. 820, will be executed . . . . tion.

849. The colonel will halt the column the moment the third division shall have its distance. As soon as the column is halted, the dispositions indicated, No. 819, will be executed, and when these are completed, the colonel may proceed to form square.

850. If the column be in march, he will also, in the first place, cause company distance to be taken, and, for this purpose, will command:

1. *To form square.* 2. *By the head of column, take half distance.* 3. March (or *double quick*—March).

851. This movement will be executed as prescribed, No. 330, and following. What is prescribed, No 820, will be executed as the first and second divisions are put in motion.

852. The colonel will proceed to form square the moment the third division shall have its distance, at the command *form square*, the dispositions indicated, No. 819, will be executed. If it be intended merely to *dispose the column for square*, the colonel will not halt the column until the last division has its distance.

853. In a simple column, left in front, these several movements will be executed according to the same principles and by inverse means, but the fronts of the square will have the same designations as if the right of the column were in front, that is, the first division will constitute the first front, and thus of the other subdivisions.

854. The battalion being formed into square, when the colonel shall wish to cause it to advance a distance of less than thirty paces, he will command:

1. *By* (such) *front, forward.* 2. March.

855. If it be supposed that the advance be made by the first front, the chief of this front will command:

1. *First division, forward.* 2. *Guide center.*

856. The chief of the second front will face his front to the left. The captains of the companies composing this front will place themselves outside, and on the right of their left guides, who will replace them in the front rank; the chief of the third front will face his front to the right, and the captains in this front will place themselves outside, and on the left of their covering sergeants; the chief of the fourth front will face his front about, and command: 1. *Fourth division, forward*, 2. *Guide center.* The captain who is in the center of the first front, will be charged with the direction of the march, and will regulate himself by the means indicated in the School of the Company, No. 89.

857. At the command *march*, the square will put itself in motion, the companies marching by the flank will be careful not to lose their distances. The chief of the fourth division will cause his division to keep constantly closed on the flanks of the second and third fronts.

858. This movement will only be executed in quick time.

SCHOOL OF THE BATTALION. 179

859. The lieutenant-colonel will place himself in rear of the file of direction in order to regulate his march.

860. If the colonel should wish to halt the square, he will command:

1. *Battalion.* 2. HALT.

861. At the second command, the square will halt; the fourth front will face about immediately, and without further command; the second and third fronts will face outwards; the captains of companies will resume their places as in square.

862. In moving the square forward by the second, third, or fourth fronts, the same rules will be observed.

863. The battalion being formed into square, when the colonel shall wish to cause it to advance a greater distance than thirty paces, he will command:

1. *Form column.*

864. The chief of the first front will command:

1. *First division forward.* 2. *Guide left.*

865. The commander of the fourth front will caution it to stand fast; the commander of the second front will cause it to face to the left, and then command, *By company, by file left.* The commander of the third front will cause it to face to the right, and then command, *By company, by file right.* At the moment the second and third fronts face to the left and right, each captain will cause to break to the rear the two leading files of his company.

866. These dispositions being made, the colonel will command:

3. MARCH (or *double quick*—MARCH).

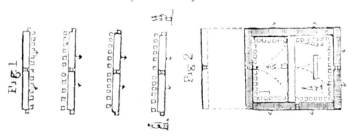

867. At this command, the first front will march forward; its chief will halt it when it shall have advanced a space equal to half its front, and align it by the left.

868. The corresponding companies of the second and third fronts will wheel by file to the left and right, and march to meet each other behind the center of the first division, and the moment they unite, the captain of each company will halt his company and face it to the front. The division being re-formed, its chief will align it by the left.

869. The commander of the fourth front will cause it to face about; its file closers will remain before the front rank

870. The column being thus re-formed, the colonel may put it in march by the commands and means prescribed, No. 164, and following, the right guides will preserve company distance exactly as the directing guides.

871. When the colonel shall wish to re-form square, he will give the commands indicated, No. 840.

872 To cause the square to march in retreat a distance greater than thirty paces, the colonel will first cause column to be formed as indicated, No. 863, and when formed, he will cause it to face by the rear rank; to this end, he will command·

1. *To march in retreat.* 2. *Face by the rear rank* 3. *Battalion, about*—FACE.

873 At the second command, the file closers of the interior divisions will place themselves, passing by the outer flanks of their respective companies, behind the front rank opposite to their places in line of battle; the file closers of the other divisions will stand fast.

874 At the third command, the battalion will face about, each chief of division will place himself before its rear rank, become front, passing through the interval between its two companies; the guides will step into the rear rank, now front.

875 The column being thus disposed, the colonel may put it in march, or cause it to form square as if it were faced by the front The square being formed, its fronts will preserve the same designations they had when faced by the front rank

876. The battalion being in square by the rear rank, when the colonel shall wish to march it in retreat or in advance, a distance less than thirty paces, he will conform to what is prescribed, No 854, and following; otherwise, he will re-form the column according to the principles prescribed, No. 863, by marching toward the fourth front

877. If the square is to be marched to the front a distance greater than thirty paces, the colonel will face the column by the front rank, to this end, he will command

1. *To march in advance* 2. *Face by the front rank.* 3 *Battalion, about*—FACE.

878. Which will be executed as prescribed, No 873, and following.

879. If the column be marching in advance, and the colonel shall wish to march it in retreat, he will command

1. *To march in retreat* 2 *Battalion, right about.* 3 MARCH (or *double quick*—MARCH).

880. At the second command, the file closers of the second and third divisions will place themselves rapidly before the front rank of their respective divisions At the command *march*, the column will face about and move off to the rear, the chiefs of divisions and the guides will conform to what is prescribed, No. 874

SCHOOL OF THE BATTALION. 181

881. If the column be marching in retreat, and the colonel shall wish to march it in advance, he will command:

1. *To march in advance.* 2. *Battalion, right about.* 3. March (or double quick—March).

882. At the second command, the file closers of the second and third divisions will place themselves before the rear rank of their respective divisions; at the third, the column will face by the front rank.

To reduce the square.

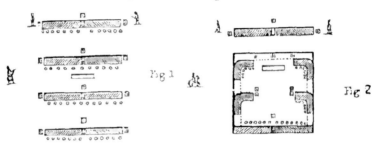

883. The colonel, wishing to break the square, will command:

1. *Reduce square.* 2. March (or *double quick*—March).

884. This movement will be executed in the manner indicated, No. 863, and following; but the file closers of the fourth front will place themselves behind the rear rank the moment it faces about; the field and staff, the color-bearer, and buglers, will, at the same time, return to their places in column.

To form square from line of battle.

885. A battalion deployed, may be formed into square in a direction either parallel or perpendicular to the line of battle.

886. In the first case, the colonel will cause the battalion to break by division to the rear, by the right or left, and then close the column to half distance, as indicated, No. 817, and following.

887. In the second case, he will ploy the battalion into simple column by division at half distance in rear of the right or left division, or into column doubled on the center.

888. To ploy the battalion into column upon one of the flank divisions, the colonel will command:

1. *To form square.* 2. *Column at half distance by division.* 3. **On** *the first (or fourth) division.* 4. *Battalion, right (or left)*—Face. 5. March (or *double quick*—March).

889. This movement will be executed according to the principles prescribed No. 119 and following.

890. If the battalion be marching in line of battle, and the colo-

nel shall wish to form square in a direction perpendicular to the line of battle, he will command

1. *To form square.* 2. *On the first (or fourth) division, form column.* 3. *Battalion, by the right (or left) flank.* 4. MARCH (or *double quick—*MARCH).

891. This movement will be executed according to the principles prescribed for ploying a column by division at half distance, No. 150. The chief of the first division will halt his division at the command *march.*

892. To ploy the battalion into double column, the colonel will command:

1. *To form square.* 2. *Double column at half distance.* 3. *Battalion, inwards—*FACE. 4. MARCH (or *double quick—*MARCH).

893. This movement will be executed as prescribed, No. 778, and following.

894. The battalion being in march, to ploy it into double column to form square, the colonel will command

1. *To form square.* 2. *Form double column.* 3. *Battalion by the right and left flanks.* 4. MARCH (or *double quick—*MARCH)

895. This movement will be executed as prescribed, No. 788. The chief of the leading division will halt his division at the command *march.*

Observations relative to the formation of squares in two ranks.

896. When the colonel shall judge it proper to have a reserve, this reserve, in a column of three divisions, will be formed of the inner platoons of the second division. The second division will, in this case, close to platoon distance on the first division. When the square is formed, the reserve platoons will move forward a distance nearly equal to a platoon front.

897. In re-forming column, the first division will move forward platoon, instead of company distance.

898. If the column be formed of four divisions, the inner platoons of the third division will compose the reserve; then, in re-forming column, the first division will conform to the general rule, and the chief of the third, as soon as his division is formed, will close it to platoon distance on the second division. The colonel may, if necessary, form the reserve of the entire third division. In this case, the movement will be executed in the following manner:

899. If the column be at full distance, when it shall close, at the command *to form square,* to half distance, the chief of the third division will cause four files to break to the rear from the right and left of his division, the guides will close upon the outer files remaining in line, and the left guide will march exactly in the trace of the file immediately in front of him. This division will then close in mass on the second division; and the chief of the fourth division will close to half distance on the same division.

900. At the command *form square*, the chief of the reserve division will command, 1. *Third division, forward.* 2. *Guide center;* at this command, the guides on the flanks will fall into the line of file closers. At the command *march*, the reserve will move forward the distance of a company front. When halted, its chief will cause the platoons to be doubled, and for this purpose will command:

1. *On the center double platoons.* 2. MARCH.

901. At the first command, the chiefs of platoon will place themselves in front of the center of their respective platoons; the chief of each outer platoon will face his platoon toward the center, and cause to break to the rear two files from the left or right. At the command *march*, the outer platoons will direct their march so as to double on the center platoon at the distance of four paces; their chiefs will align these outer platoons on the center, and the files previously broken to the rear will come into line.

902. If the column be at half, instead of full distance, the colonel before forming square will order the chiefs of the third and fourth divisions to move forward their divisions as prescribed No. 899.

903. If the column be closed in mass, at the command *to form square*, the chief of the third division will break four files to the rear from each of the flanks, as prescribed No. 899.

904. The colonel will halt the column as soon as the second division shall have gained its distance.

905. If the colonel shall wish the column to continue marching, at the command, *By the head of column take half distance*, the chief of the reserve division will give his cautionary commands in sufficient time to place his division in motion, simultaneously with the one which precedes it. The chief of the fourth division will give the command *march*, at the instant there is company distance between his division and the second.

906. When the colonel shall wish to re-form the column, at the command *form column*, the chief of the third division will command, *Form division;* at this command, the chiefs of the outer platoons which have doubled in rear of the center platoons, will give the commands and make the preparatory movements for deploying on the center platoons, which will be executed at the command *march*, given by the colonel and briskly repeated by the chief of this division. The division being re-formed, the chiefs of the outer platoons will retake their places in column, and the chief of this division will again cause four files from each of its flanks to break to the rear.

907. If, before the formation of the square, the column had been left in front, it would be formed by the same commands and according to the same principles. The second division, in this case, would form the reserve.

908. Th[illegible] wish to march [illegible] files of

the third division broken off to the rear, will face about with the battalion, and, when the column is put in motion, will march in front of the rear rank. But, should the colonel wish to re-form the square, he will cause the battalion to face by the front rank

909 If the battalion be in line, instead of in column, the chief of the reserve division will bring it into column in such manner that there may be a distance of only four paces between this division and the one which is to be immediately in front of it; and when this division is halted and aligned, its chief will cause the usual number of files to be broken to the rear. The chief of the division which should occupy in column a position immediately in rear of the reserve division will, on entering the column, take a distance of twelve paces between it and the division established immediately in front of the reserve division.

Squares in four ranks.

910 If the square formed in two ranks, according to the preceding rules, should not be deemed sufficiently strong, the colonel may cause the square to be formed in four ranks.

911 The battalion being in column by company at full distance right in front, and at a halt, when the colonel shall wish to form square in four ranks, he will first cause divisions to be formed, which being executed, he will command

1. *To form square in four ranks.* 2. *To half distance, close column.*
    3 MARCH (or *double quick*—MARCH)

912 At the first command, the chief of the first division will caution the right company to face to the left, and the left company to face to the right. The chiefs of the other divisions will caution their divisions to move forward

913 At the command *march*, the right company of the first division will form into four ranks on its left file, and the left company into four ranks on its right file. The formation ended, the chief of this division will align it by the left

914 The other divisions will move forward and double their files marching; the right company of each division will double on its left file, and the left company on its right file. The formation completed, each chief of division will command, *Guide left*. Each chief will halt his division when it shall have the distance of a company front in four ranks from the preceding one, counting from its rear rank, and will align his division by the left. At the instant the fourth division is halted, the file closers will move rapidly before its front rank.

915. The colonel will form square, re-form column, and reduce square in four ranks, by the same commands and means as prescribed for a battalion in two ranks.

916. If the square formed in four ranks be reduced and at a halt, and the colonel shall wish to form the battalion into two ranks, he will command.

SCHOOL OF THE BATTALION. 185

1. *In two ranks undouble files.* 2. *Battalion outwards*—FACE.
3. MARCH.

917. At the first command, the captains will step before the centers of their respective companies, and those on the right will caution them to face to the right, and those on the left to face to the left.

918. At the second command, the battalion will face to the right and left.

919. At the command *march*, each company will undouble its files and re-form into two ranks as indicated in the school of the company No. 376, and following. Each captain will halt his company and face it to the front. The formation completed, each chief of division will align his division by the left.

920. If the column be in march, with divisions formed in four ranks, and the colonel shall wish to re-form them into two ranks, he will command.

1. *Guide center.* 2. *In two ranks, undouble files.* 3. MARCH.

921. The captain, placed in the center of each division, will continue to march straight to the front, as will also the left file of the right company, and the right file of the left company. Each company will then be re-formed into two ranks, as prescribed in the school of the company.

922. The battalion being formed into two ranks, the colonel will command, *Guide left* (or *right*).

923. To form square in four ranks on one of the flank divisions, the colonel will command:

1. *To form square, in four ranks.* 2. *Column at half distance, by division.* 3. *On the first* (or *fourth*) *division.* 4. *Battalion, right* (or *left*)—FACE. 5. MARCH (or *double quick*—MARCH).

924. At the second command, each chief of division will place himself before the center of his division, and caution it to face to the right.

925. At the fourth command, the right guide of the first division will remain faced to the front, the battalion will face to the right.

926. At the command *march*, the first file of four men of the first division will face to the front remaining doubled. All the other files of four men will step off together, and each in succession will close up to its proper distance on the file preceding it, and face to the front, remaining doubled. When the last file shall have closed, the chief of division will command, *Left*—DRESS.

927. The other divisions will ploy into column in the same manner as with a battalion in two ranks, observing what follows, the chiefs of division, instead of allowing their divisions to file past them on entering the column, will continue to lead them, and as each division shall arrive on a line with the right guide of the first division, ... ediately

face to the front; the first file of four men will also halt at the same time and face to the front, remaining doubled. The second file will close on the first, and when closed, halt, and face to the front, remaining doubled. All the other files will execute successively what has just been prescribed for the second. When the last file shall have closed, the chief of division will command, *Left*—Dress.

928. If the battalion be in march, the colonel will command:

1. *To form square, in four ranks.* 2. *On the first division, form column* 3. *Battalion. by the right flank.* 4. March (or *double quick*—March).

929 At the second command, each chief of division will step in front of the center of his division and caution it to face by the right flank The chief of the first division will caution his covering sergeant to halt, and remain faced to the front.

930. At the command *march*, the battalion will face to the right, the covering sergeant of the first division will halt and remain faced to the front, the first division will then form into four ranks as heretofore prescribed The other divisions will ploy into column in the same manner as if the movement had taken place from a halt

931 If the colonel should wish to form a perpendicular square in four ranks, by double column, he will command·

1. *To form square, in four ranks* 2 *Double column, at half distance.* 3 *Battalion inwards*— Face. 4. March (or *double quick*— March)

932 At the second command, the captains of companies will place themselves before the centers of their respective companies, and caution those on the right to face to the left, and those on the left to face to the right. The captain of the fifth company will caution his covering sergeant to stand fast

933 At the third command, the battalion will face to the left and right, at the command *march*, the left file of the fourth, and the right file of the fifth company, will face to the front, remaining doubled. The fourth company will close successively by file of fours on the left file, and the fifth company, in like manner, on the right file, the files will face to the front, remaining doubled. The formation completed, the chief of division will command, *Right dress*. The junior captain will place himself in the interval between the two companies.

934. The other companies will close as prescribed for the double column in two ranks, observing what follows: each captain will halt the leading guide of his company the moment the head of his company arrives on a line with the center of the column In the right companies, the left guides will step into the line of file closers, and the left file of four men will face immediately to the front, remaining doubled, and by the side of the right guide of the left company. The companies will each form into four ranks, as pre-

SCHOOL OF THE BATTALION. 187

scribed No. 926, the right companies on the left file, and the left companies on the right file. The formation completed, the junior captain will place himself between the two companies, and the senior will command, *Right dress.*

935. If the battalion be in march, the colonel will command:

1. *To form square, in four ranks.* 2. *Form double column.* 3. *Battalion by the right and left flanks.* 4. MARCH (or *double quick*—MARCH.

936. At the second command, the captains will place themselves before the centers of their respective companies, and those on the right will caution them to face by the left flank, and those on the left to face by the right flank; the captain of the fifth company will caution his covering sergeant to halt, and remain faced to the front.

937. At the command *march*, the fourth and fifth companies will halt. The battalion will face to the left and right; the covering sergeant of the fifth company will halt and remain faced to the front, the movement will then be executed as if the battalion was at a halt.

Oblique squares.

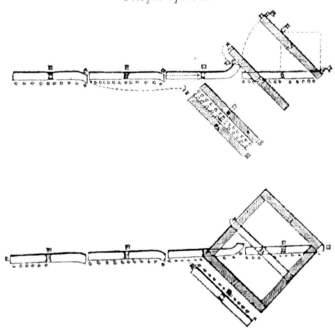

938. The battalion being in line of battle, when the colonel shall wish to form the oblique square, he will command:

1. *To form oblique square.* 2. *On the first division form column.*

939. At the second command the lieutenant colonel will trace the alignment of the first division in the following manner: he

will place himself before and near the right file of this division, face to the left, march twelve paces along the front rank, halt, face to the right, march twelve paces perpendicularly to the front, halt again, face to the right, and immediately place a marker at this point. The covering sergeant of the right company will step, at the same time, before its right file, face to the left, and conform the line of his shoulders to that of the shoulders of the marker established by the lieutenant-colonel. These two markers being established, the lieutenant-colonel will place a third marker on the same alignment, at the point where the left of the division will halt.

940. The chiefs of division will place themselves in front of the centers of their divisions; the chief of the first division will immediately establish it by a wheel to the right on a fixed pivot, against the markers, and align it by the left. The chiefs of the other divisions will caution them to face to the right. The colonel will then command

3. *Battalion right*—FACE   4. MARCH (or *double quick*—MARCH).

941. The three rear divisions will direct their march so as to place themselves at half distance from each other, and in the rear of the first division, as previously indicated, observing what follows:

942. The chief of the second division, instead of breaking the headmost files to the rear, will break them to the front, and at the command *march*, will conduct his division towards the point of entrance into the column. Arrived at this point, he will halt in his own person, cause his division to wheel by file to the right, instructing the right guide to direct himself parallelly to the first division, and as soon as the left file has passed, its chief will halt the division, and align it by the left. The other divisions will break to the rear, but slightly; each will enter the column as prescribed for the second, and the moment the battalion is ployed into column, the colonel will cause it to form square.

943. The formation of a battalion into oblique square on the left division, will be executed according to the same principles and by inverse means.

944. Should the battalion be in march, the colonel will first cause it to halt.

945. In the preceding example, the battalion was supposed to be deployed; but if it be already formed in column, the desired obliquity will be established by causing it to change direction by the flank, to this end, the colonel will command:

1. *To form oblique square.* 2. *Change direction by the right (or left) flank.*

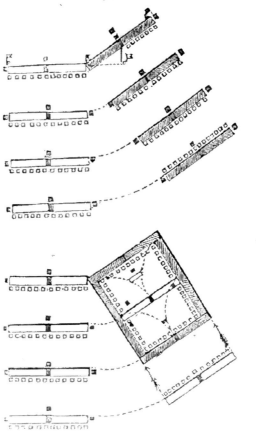

946. At the second command, the lieutenant-colonel will trace the new direction in the following manner; he will place before the right and left files of the headmost division, two markers, and a third on the prolongation of the first two, on the side of the change of direction, and at twelve paces from the flank of the column. He will then place himself before the third marker, march twelve paces perpendicularly to the front, halt, and finish tracing the new direction in the manner indicated, No. 939.

947. The colonel will then command:

3. *Battalion right (or left)*—FACE. 4. MARCH (or *double quick*—MARCH.)

948. The change of direction having been executed, the colonel will cause the square to be formed.

949. Should the column be in march, the colonel will first cause it to halt

950. Oblique squares in four ranks, will be executed by the same means, and according to the principles prescribed for the formation of squares in four ranks.

951. Whether the battalion be ployed into simple or double column, the particular dispositions for the formation of the square will be executed as prescribed No. 819 and following. The division which is to form the rear of the column, will be closed in mass, and as soon as it is aligned, the major will rectify the position of the guides on the side of the column opposite to the direction.

952. If it be the wish of the colonel merely to prepare for square, he will in all formations with that view substitute the command *prepare for square* in place of *to form square*, and in that case, the last division will enter the column at company distance.

Remarks on the formation of squares.

953. It is a general principle that a column by company, which is to be formed into square, will first form divisions, and close to half distance. Nevertheless, if it find itself suddenly threatened by cavalry without sufficient time to form divisions, the colonel will cause the column to close to platoon distance and then form square by the commands and means which have been indicated, the leading and rearmost companies will conform themselves to what has been prescribed for divisions in those positions. The other companies will form by platoon to the right and left into line of battle, and each chief of platoon, after having halted it, will place himself on the line, as if the platoon were a company, and he will be covered by the guide in the rear rank.

954. A battalion in column at full distance, having to form square, will always close on the leading subdivision; and a column closed in mass, will always, for the same purpose, take distances by the head. In either case, the second subdivision should be careful, in taking its distance, to reckon from the rear rank of the subdivision in front of it.

955. If a column by company should be required to form square in four ranks, the doubling of files will always take place on the file next the guide.

956. When a column, disposed to form square, shall be in march, it will change direction as a column at half distance; thus, having to execute this movement, the column will take the guide on the side opposite to that to which the change of direction is to be made, if *that* be not already the side of the guide.

957. A column doubled on the center at company distance or closed in mass, may be formed into square according to the same principles as a simple column.

958. When a battalion is ployed, with a view to the square, it will always be in rear of the right or left division, in order that it may be able to commence firing, pending the execution of the movement. The double column, also, affords this advantage, and being more promptly formed than any other, it will habitually be

employed, unless particular circumstances cause a different formation to be preferred.

959. A battalion, in square, will never use any other than the fire by file and by rank; the color being in the line of file closers, its guard will not fall back as prescribed No. 41; it will fire like the men of the company of which it forms a part.

960. If the square be formed in four ranks, the first two ranks will alone execute the firings prescribed above; the other two ranks will remain either at shoulder or support arms.

961. The formation of the square being often necessary in war, and being the most complicated of the manœuvres, it will be as frequently repeated as the supposed necessity may require, in order to render its mechanism familiar to both officers and men.

962. In the execution of this manœuvre, the colonel will carefully observe that the divers movements which it involves succeed each other without loss of time, but also without confusion; for, if the rapidity of cavalry movements requires the greatest promptitude in the formation of squares, so, on the other hand, precipitancy always results in disorder, and in no circumstance is disorder more to be avoided.

963. When the colonel shall wish to cover by skirmishers the movements of a column preparing to form square, he will detach for this purpose one or two inner platoons of one of the interior divisions of the column. In this case, the exterior platoons of this division and the following subdivisions, will, according to circumstances, close on the preceding subdivision, in such manner, that there may be between them only the distance necessary for forming into line.

964. When the colonel shall be ready to form square, he will, in order to recall the skirmishers, cause *to the color* to be sounded. If on the return of the skirmishers, there be not room for them to form into line of battle, they will double on the outer platoons of their respective companies.

Column against Cavalry.

965. When a column closed in mass has to form square, it will begin by ta...

by cavalry as not to allow time for this disposition, it will be formed in the following manner

966 The colonel will command:

1. *Column against Cavalry* 2 MARCH

967 At the first command, the chief of the leading division will caution it to stand fast and pass behind the rear rank, in the interior divisions each captain will promptly designate the number of files necessary to close the interval between his company and the one in front of it. The captains of the divisions next to the one in rear, in addition to closing the interval in front, will also close up the interval which separates this division from the last, the chief of the fourth division will caution it to face about, and its file closers will pass briskly before the front rank.

968 At the command *march*, the guides of each division will place themselves rapidly in the line of file closers. The first division will stand fast, the fourth will face about, the outer file of each of these divisions will then face outwards; in the other divisions the files designated for closing the intervals will form to the right and left into line, but in the division next to the rearmost one, the first files that come into line will close to the right or left until they join the rear division. The files of each company which remain in column will close on their outer files, formed into line, in order to create a vacant space in the middle of the column.

969. If the column be in march, the *column against cavalry* will be formed by the same commands and means. At the command *march*, the first and fourth divisions will halt and the latter division will face about; the interior divisions will conform to what has been prescribed above.

970. The battalion being no longer threatened by cavalry, the colonel will command:

1 *Form column* 2 MARCH

971 At the command *march*, the files in column will close to the left and right to make room for those in line, who will retake their places in column by stepping backwards, except those closing the interval between the two rear divisions, who will take their places in column by a flank movement. The fourth division will face about, the guides will resume their places.

972 If the colonel should be so pressed as not to have time to order bayonets to be fixed, the men will fix them, without command or signal, at the cautionary command, *column against cavalry*

973 As this manœuvre is often used in war, and with decided advantage, the colonel will frequently cause it to be executed, in order to render it familiar

ARTICLE XV.—*The rally*

974 The battalion, being in line of battle, the colonel will sometimes cause the disperse to be sounded, at which signal the battalion will break and disperse.

SCHOOL OF THE BATTALION.

975. When the colonel shall wish to rally the battalion, he will cause *to the color* to be sounded, and at the same time place two markers and the color-bearer in the direction he may wish to give the battalion.

976. Each captain will rally his company about six paces in rear of the place it is to occupy in line of battle.

977. The colonel will cause the color-company to be promptly established against the markers, and each company by the command of its captain will be aligned on the color-company, according to the principles heretofore prescribed.

978. When the colonel shall wish to rally the battalion in column, he will cause *the assembly* to be sounded, and place two markers before the position to be occupied by the first company; the captain of this company will rally his company in rear of the two markers, and each of the other captains will rally his company at platoon distance, behind the one which should precede it in the order in the column.

ARTICLE XVI.—*Rules for manœuvring by the rear rank.*

979. It may often be necessary to cause a battalion to manœuvre by the rear rank; when the case presents itself, the following rules will be observed.

980. The battalion being by the front rank, when the colonel shall wish to manœuvre by the rear rank, he will command:

1. *Face by the rear rank.* 2. *Battalion.* 3. *About*—FACE.

981. If the battalion be deployed, this movement will be executed as has been indicated for the fire by the rear rank.

982. If the battalion be in column by company, or by platoon, right or left in front, the chiefs of subdivision, to take their new and front, will each pass by the left flank of his subdivi-

194 SCHOOL OF THE BATTALION.

rear rank is deployed, the subdivisions which, in line of battle by the front rank, ought to find themselves on the right of the subdivision on which the deployment is made, will face to the left; and those which ought to be placed on its left, will face to the right.

988. When a battalion in line of battle, faced by the rear rank, is to be ployed into column, the colonel will announce in the commands, *left* or *right in front*, according as it may be intended that the first or last subdivision shall be at the head of the column, because the first subdivision is on the left, and the last on the right of the battalion faced by the rear rank. The column by the rear rank will take the guide to the right, if the first subdivision be in front, and to the left in the reverse case.

989. A column, faced by the rear rank, will be brought to its proper front by the means heretofore prescribed. If the column be formed by company, or by platoon, the chiefs of subdivision, in order to take their new places in column, will pass by the left of subdivisions, now right, and the file closers by the right, now left.

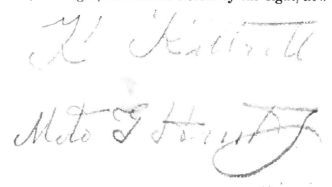

1. *Form column.* 2. MARCH.

971. At the command *march*, the files in column will close to the left and right to make room for those in line, who will retake their places in column by stepping backwards, except those closing the interval between the two rear divisions, who will take their places in column by a flank movement. The fourth division will face about, the guides will resume their places.

972. If the colonel should be so pressed as not to have time to order bayonets to be fixed, the men will fix them, without command or signal, at the cautionary command, *column against cavalry*.

973. As this manœuvre is often used in war, and with decided advantage, the colonel will frequently cause it to be executed, in order to render it familiar.

ARTICLE XV.—*The rally.*

974. The battalion, being in line of battle, the colonel will sometimes cause the disperse to be sounded, at which signal the battalion will break and disperse.

TABLE OF CONTENTS.

TITLE FIRST.

ARTICLE FIRST

Formation of a regiment in order of battle, or in line	3
Posts of company officers, sergeants and corporals	4
Posts of field officers and regimental staff	4
Posts of field music and band	5
Color-guard	5
General guides	6

ARTICLE SECOND

Instruction of the battalion	6
Instruction of officers	7
Instruction of sergeants	7
Instruction of corporals	8
Commands	8

TITLE SECOND—SCHOOL OF THE SOLDIER.

PART FIRST

General rules and division of the school of the soldier	8
Lesson I.—Position of the soldier (No. 78.) Eyes right, left and front (Nos. 80, 83)	10
Lesson II.—Facings (Nos. 88, 91)	12
Lesson III.—Principles of the direct step in common and quick time (Nos. 94, 102)	12
Lesson IV.—Principles of the double quick step (No. 104)	13

PART SECOND

General rules	14
Lesson I.—Principles of shouldered arms	15
Lesson II.—Manual of arms. Support arms (No. 133.) Present arms (No. 143.) Order arms (No. 147.) Position of order arms (No. 149.) Load in nine times (No. 156.) Ready (No. 171.) Aim (No. 174.) Fire (No. 177.) Fix bayonet (No. 188.) Charge bayonet (No. 193.) Trail arms (No. 197.) Unfix bayonet (No. 200.) Secure arms (No. 204.) Right shoulder shift arms (No. 210.) Arms at will (No. 219.) Ground arms (No. 222.) Inspection arms (No. 227.) Remarks on the manual of arms (No. 237.) Mark time (No. 241.) Change step (No. 245.)	

March backwards (No. 247.)	15
Lesson III.—Load in four times (No. 250.) Load at will (No. 257.)	28
Lesson IV.—Firings. Direct fire (No. 261.) Oblique firings (No. 266.) Position of the two ranks in the oblique fire to the right (No 267.) Position of the two ranks in the oblique fire to the left (No. 270.) Fire by file (No. 275.) Fire by rank (No. 285.)	29
Lesson V.—Fire and load kneeling (No. 292.) Fire and load, lying (No. 300.)	31
Lesson VI.—Bayonet exercise	33

PART THIRD.

Lesson I.—Alignments	34
Lesson II.—March by the front (No. 325.) March by the front in double quick time (No. 334.) Face about in marching (No. 343.) March backwards (No. 345.)	35
Lesson III.—March by the flank (No. 351.) March by the flank in double quick time (No. 368.)	38
Lesson IV.—General principles of wheeling (No. 377.) Wheeling from a halt (No. 383.) Wheeling in marching (No. 393.) Turning (No. 400.) Wheeling and turning in double quick time (No. 403.)	40
Lesson V.—Long marches in double quick time and the run (No. 406.) Stack arms (No. 410.) Take arms (No. 413.)	43

TITLE THIRD—SCHOOL OF THE COMPANY.

General rules and division of the school of the company	45

LESSON FIRST.

Article I.—To open ranks (No. 8.)	46
Article II.—Alignments in open ranks (No. 18.)	47
Article III.—Manual of arms (No. 26.)	48
Article IV.—To close ranks (No. 28.)	48
Article V.—Alignments, and manual of arms in closed ranks (No. 30)	49

LESSON SECOND.

Article I.—To load in four times and at will (No. 44)	50
Article II.—To fire by company (No. 48)	50
Article III.—To fire by file (No. 55).	51
Article IV.—To fire by rank (No. 58)	51
Article V.—To fire by the rear rank (No. 68)	52

LESSON THIRD.

Article I.—To advance in line of battle (No. 84)	53
Article II.—To halt the company marching in line of battle, and to align it (No. 99)	55
Article III.—Oblique march in line of battle (No. 101)	55
Article IV.—To mark time, to march in double quick time, and the back step (No. 109.)	56

TABLE OF CONTENTS.

Article V.—To march in retreat (No 119)	57

LESSON FOURTH

Article I.—To march by the flank (No. 135)	59
Article II—To change direction by file (No. 142)	60
Article III—To halt the company, marching by the flank, and to face it to the front (No. 145)	60
Article IV—The company being in march by the flank, to form it on the right or left, by file into line of battle (No. 148)	61
Article V.—The company marching by the flank, to form it by company or platoon into line, and cause it to face to the right and left in marching (No. 153)	62

LESSON FIFTH

Article I.—To break into column by platoon, either at a halt or marching (No 171)	64
Article II—To march in column (No 195)	67
Article III—To change direction (No 211)	69
Article IV—To halt the column (No 231)	71
Article V.—Being in column by platoon, to form to the right or left into line of battle, either at a halt, or marching (No. 235).	72

LESSON SIXTH

Article I.—To break the company into platoons, and to re-form the company (No 265)	75
Article II—To break files to the rear and to cause them to re-enter into line (No 289)	77
Article III—To march in column in route, and to execute the movements incident thereto (No 306)	79
Article IV—Countermarch (No 334)	82
Article V—Being in column by platoon, to form on the right or left into line of battle (No 343)	83
Formation of a company from two ranks into single ranks, and reciprocally (No 359)	85
Formation of a company from two ranks into four, and reciprocally, at a halt, and marching (No 371)	86

TITLE FOURTH—SCHOOL OF THE BATTALION.

Formation of the battalion (No. 1)	91
Composition and march of the color-escort (No 4)	91
Honors paid to the color (No 11)	92
General rules and division of the school of the battalion (No 14)	92

PART FIRST.

Article I—To open and close ranks (No. 22)	93
Article II.—Manual of arms (No. 30)	93
Article III.—Loading at will, and the firings (No 31)	94

PART SECOND.

Article I—To break by company to the right (No 69). Break by company to the left (No 74) Break by division (No

75). To break by company, marching (No. 84)............ 97
Article II.—Break to the rear by the right or left of companies (No. 87). Break to the rear by the right or left of com-companies, marching (No. 94). Advance or retire by the right or left of companies (No. 105). Advance or retire by the right or left of companies, marching (No. 110). Advancing or retiring by the right or left of companies, to form line to the front (No. 113).......................... 99
Article III.—Ploy the battalion into close column on the first division (No. 119). Ploy the battalion into close column on the fourth division (No. 141). Ploy the battalion into close column on any interior division (No. 143). Battalion being in march, to ploy it into column on the first division (No. 149).. 103

PART THIRD.

Article I.—March in column at full distance (No. 164). Column being in march, to execute the about (No. 170). Column arriving in front of the line of battle, to prolong it on this line (No. 175). Column arriving behind the line of battle, to prolong it on this line (No. 184). Column arriving on the right or left of the line of battle, to prolong it on this line (No. 188). Manner of prolonging a line by markers (No. 189).. 108
Article III.—Change of direction in column at full distance (No 231)... 112
Article IV.—Halt the column (No. 239) 113
Article V—Close the column to half distance, or in mass (No. 252). Close the column on the eighth company (No. 267). Execute this movement marching (No. 273).................. 114
Article VI.—March in column at half distance, or closed in mass (No. 281).. 116
Article VII.—Change direction in column at half distance (No. 287)... 117
Article VIII.—Change direction of a column closed in mass, marching (No. 288). Change direction of a column, closed in mass, from a halt (No. 306)............................... 117
Article IX.—Take distances by the head of the column (No. 323). Take distances by the rear of the column (No. 333). Take distances on the head of the column (No. 341)... 121
Article X.—Countermarch of a column at full or half distance (No. 351). Countermarch of a column closed in mass (No. 352)... 125
Article XI.—Being in column by company, closed in mass, to form divisions (No. 364). To form divisions, marching (No. 376)... 126

PART FOURTH.

Article II.—To form a column, at full distance, to the left into

CPSIA information can be obtained at www.ICGtesting.com
Printed in the USA
BVOW02s1142251114

376672BV00003B/6/P